A NEW LOOK at Microwave Cooking A practical guide to the possibilities of your Microwave Oven

By Lila Chalpin

dhp

Dorison House Publishers, Boston

Illustrations by Calvin Burnett

Copyright © 1976 by Dorison House Publishers, Inc.

Published by Dorison House Publishers, Inc.
824 Park Square Building, Boston, Massachusetts 02116

ISBN: 0-916752-04-6

Library of Congress Catalog Card Number: 76-41-144

Manufactured in the United States of America

Eleventh Printing   *March*   *1982*

Contents

Acknowledgments

There are several people whose help in preparing this book has been invaluable.

Anne Howard, Director of Home Economics at Sharp Electronics Corporation, instructed me in the basics and idiosyncracies of microwaves. She and members of her staff, read every centimeter of this book and commented on it with tact, patience, and infinite wisdom.

G. Alda Spencer, Interior Designer, applied her creativity and verve to this book with all the magic of a microwave. She contributed not only many recipes but also other uses of the oven. I shall miss those midnight visits of hers laden with a basket of delights to sample and critique.

Marilyn Kostick, dietician and editor, lent both her expertise and support whenever needed.

My mother, Esther Price, gifted me at an early age with her contagious enthusiasm for food preparation.

My three children, Mark the gourmand, Lorna, the candy-maker, and David, the gourmet, after all these years of my feeding them, have now given me feedback.

My friends generously shared scientific knowledge, treasured recipes, and tastebuds with me.

Lila Chalpin

About The Author

Lila Chalpin was born in Boston and educated at the University of Wisconsin. She is Assistant Professor of Literature and Creative Writing at Massachusetts College of Art, a writer of innumerable articles, stories, and poems, and an editor of an anthology, Achievements in Fiction. Cooking to her is not only a matter of survival with three children but also an act of levitation that raises her above daily banalities and tensions.

Preface

This book is much more than a cookbook. It is meant to serve as a practical guide to the everyday use of your microwave oven. Many kitchen-tested recipes are included, but in addition, there are ideas and hints to encourage you to use your microwave oven to its fullest potential.

Quick reference charts will help you in the cooking of convenience foods. Many of the mixes, dehydrated products and quick-cook items found on grocery store shelves can be prepared by microwave cooking, but only if you know how and how long. Handy reference charts for cooking all types of frozen foods and reheating foods are also included.

You can convert your own favorite recipes so that they will work well in your microwave oven. Follow the guidelines in this book, and your mother's old-fashioned meat loaf recipe will be just as delicious as ever, but done in much less time.

In the last chapter you will find many original and unusual ideas for using your microwave oven. You'll learn to preshrink fabric, make dough ornaments or bread baskets and dry flowers, to name only a few of the unorthodox suggestions.

The most exciting new major appliance in today's kitchens, your microwave oven will save you time, energy and labor. It's so convenient it can be the most frequently used piece of equipment in your kitchen. So, take advantage of its versatility. Experiment, enjoy, and make maximum use of your microwave oven.

Introduction

CHAPTER 1

THE WONDERS OF MICROWAVE OVENS

Your microwave oven will change your lifestyle. In many instances you will find that it will take you more time to set your table or dress for dinner than to cook it!

Your microwave oven will save time
Whether you use it to supplement your other appliances or by itself, it will reduce cooking time by one-half to three-quarters. One woman, who welcomes unexpected company in the afternoon or evening, affectionately calls her oven, "the zapper." She "zaps" a frozen apple pie in and out of the oven while her guests are taking off their coats.

Your microwave oven will conserve energy
A microwave oven consumes approximately 1500 watts. This is a little more than an electric skillet consumes but less than a conventional oven. Since the microwave oven does not emit heat, your kitchen will remain cool and comfortable despite the weather or preparations.

Your microwave oven will save labor
You can say goodbye to oven cleaners that sting your eyes, sticky rubber gloves, baked-on spatters, fans and hoods to get rid of lingering odors, and scouring pads for thickly crusted pots and pans. All the oven cleaning that is necessary is a simple wipe with a damp cloth. Also, you will appreciate having fewer dishes to wash because you will often cook and serve in the same utensil.

Your microwave oven will preserve nutritional value, taste, and appearance of food.
With quicker cooking and no additional water, there is less loss of vitamins, minerals, texture, and flavor. Now you can freeze many dishes for future microwave defrosting and heating that yield the original flavor or an enhanced one.

Your microwave oven will utilize convenience foods to an even greater advantage than your conventional oven does
In this cookbook there are many charts for preparing packaged and frozen convenience foods according to swifter microwave time. In addition, there are recipes throughout using convenience foods with creativity.

HOW MICROWAVES WORK IN YOUR OVEN

Cooking with microwave energy differs from conventional energy in that there is no direct application of heat or process of heat penetration to cook the food. In conventional cooking, heat energy is absorbed slowly by the food. For example, when you bake a cake, you must not open the oven door for at least twenty minutes or the sudden change in environmental temperature, which can drop up to 50°, will cause the cake to fall. However, with a microwave oven you can open the door in the middle of baking a cake, since there is no change in environmental temperature and the cake will rise evenly. This is because the microwave oven heats food swiftly and evenly. Microwaves pass through the food in the oven quickly and cause the water molecules within the food to vibrate at extremely high speeds. This vibration acts as friction which produces the intense heat that cooks the food. We are familiar with this friction in the heat produced by rubbing two sticks together or rubbing palms together. The high speed of vibration accounts for the dramatic savings in the cooking time.

Cooking by microwaves shortens cooking time by as much as 75%. To cook food effectively, microwave energy must not be deflected within the oven. To avoid this, limit the use of metal containers or aluminum foil. Microwave energy must be allowed to pass through the utensils in order to be absorbed by the water molecules within the food and thus cook the food. The best cooking utensils are paper, glass, plastic, porcelain, china, wicker, and wood because microwaves can pass easily through them and are not deflected.

Containers, Utensils, Wraps and Covers

The perfect container for use in your microwave over should have tolerance for low and high temperatures and be made of nonmetallic material. More and more products are being manufactured especially for microwave cooking.

Paper napkins, towels, plastic wrap, wax paper, freezer paper and cardboard may be used to wrap or cover food while cooking and prevent spatters. A cotton napkin may be used in the bottom of a wicker basket while warming rolls to absorb the steam which forms between the underside of the rolls and the basket and prevent the rolls from becoming soggy.

A Simple Test

An easy way to test a container is to place it empty in the microwave oven along with 1 cup of water (to protect the oven from underload). If the container becomes hot to the touch within 30-45 seconds, do not use it.

Browning Dishes

Browning dishes made with a ferrite coating are specifically designed for use in microwave ovens. These dishes brown meats, poultry, and fish but may also be used for grilling sandwiches, baking pancakes, and frying eggs. Note Browning Chart on page 16.

Metal Utensils

Metal utensils and utensils with metallic trim, even the wire ties for plastic bags (string may be used instead), should be kept out of your microwave oven. There are two main reasons for this. Microwaves are reflected by metals; therefore, foods in metal containers will not cook so well as in plastic, glass, china or porcelain. Also, there is a possibility of a static discharge or spark between the gap in the metal of the oven and the metal utensil. This is called "arcing." If you do see this spark inside the oven, just turn the oven off and transfer the food to a nonmetallic container.

Generally, there are four exceptions when metal may be used in a microwave oven.

1) Aluminum Foil

Small amounts of aluminum foil may be used in the microwave oven for shielding. If, for example, you are cooking a turkey, and the wings begin to overcook, you can wrap small pieces of aluminum foil around the wing tips to protect the turkey from cooking more in this area. There should be a large volume of food whenever you are using metal.

2) Frozen Dinners in Foil Containers

When cooking foods in foil containers, the container should be no more than 3/4" deep. Remember that cooking in metal reflects waves away from the food. Therefore, you must remove any foil that is covering the top of the container, return the metal container to the paper box it was packaged in, and place this entire unit in the microwave oven.

3) Metal Skewers

Small metal skewers may be used if there is a large proportion of food to the amount of metal. If "arcing'" does begin, stop the oven, remove the food, and change to wooden skewers or chopsticks.

4) Microwave Oven Thermometers

Conventional metal and candy thermometers should NEVER be used in the microwave oven while it is in operation. Only specially designed microwave cooking thermometers or the temperature probe may be used when oven is in operation. If you are using a conventional thermometer, use it only *after* cooking.

Whenever using metal foil, foil containers or metal skewers, be sure that the metal does not touch the sides of the oven.

HOW TO USE THE VARIABLE COOKING CONTROLS

The new microwave ovens have five settings to allow you to select the speed at which you want your food cooked. The microwave energy turns on and off at different intervals to give you the choice of FULL (100% of power), ROAST (70% of power), SIMMER (50% of power), DEFROST (30% of power) and WARM (10% of power). After you have set the time you wish to cook or defrost, simply select the Variable Cooking Control you need. For most foods, FULL POWER or ROAST will give you good results, and they will be done in about one-fourth of their conventional times. Even those foods requiring the slower settings of SIMMER or DEFROST will be ready more quickly than they would if cooked conventionally.

Use your Variable Cooking Control to cook less tender cuts of meat, to develop flavor in stews, soups or sauces, for food such as eggs, milk, cream, cheese or sour cream that are especially sensitive to microwave energy, and to prevent overcooking.

Most Recipes in this book were successfully tested on FULL POWER in microwave ovens of 650 output wattage. If you have a smaller oven with lower wattage, cook with maximum cooking times when a range of suggested times is given. If your oven has variable power and you wish to use the reduced power setting it will be necessary to lengthen the cooking time. Refer to your Use and Care Manual. Whenever you are unsure of cooking time, undercook. Then it will be easy to adjust the time.

NOT FOR MICROWAVE COOKING

*Do not cook eggs in the shell. Pressure will build up inside the shell and it will burst. Do not reheat cooked eggs unless they are scrambled or chopped. Puncture the yolk with a toothpick or fork before cooking eggs.

*Don't use your microwave oven for foods needing a crisp crust such as popovers, puff pastries, turnovers, french bread and hard rolls, pizza (except frozen, which can be heated on a browning dish) or two-crust pies.

*It is not advisable to attempt deep fried foods such as crisp fried chicken, fish, doughnuts or french fries. The temperature of the oil is difficult to control, and there is the possibility of overheating.

*Popcorn should not be popped in paper bags or glass utensils. There are special microwave poppers with directions to be carefully followed.

*Canning is not recommended in your microwave oven.

NEW CONCEPTS IN COOKING

Since food cooked by microwaves differs in several ways from food cooked by conventional ranges and grills, it is necessary for you to reorganize habits and judgments in your food preparation.

Think time, not temperature

The amount of time needed to cook a particular food is directly related to the starting temperature of the food, its volume and its density. You will gradually learn to allow for the starting temperature of food that comes from the freezer, refrigerator, or cupboards. The volume of food increases the cooking time. One small potato cooks in 3-1/2 minutes; a medium potato cooks in 4-5 minutes; two potatoes cook in 8-9 minutes. The density of the food increases cooking time. It takes longer to cook or defrost a 1-1/2 pound piece of meat than a 1-1/2 pound loaf of bread. A casserole will cook faster spread out over a larger surface rather than heaped high in a small container.

If your oven has a temperature probe you needn't think time.

Some ovens have removable probe you can insert into a roast or casserole and set to the desired internal temperature. When the food has reached that heat, the oven automatically turns off, or can hold the food at a selected temperature.

Think time, not appearance of food

Unless you use a browning dish or conventional range, or possess a microwave oven with a built-in browner, microwave oven cooked food may not brown on top or crust at the edges as cooked food usually does. Because microwaves cook so swiftly, a piece of meat may be cooked to a medium or well-done state and still appear somewhat pink on the inside. (You will find that larger cuts of meat tend to brown without prebrowning.) Should you feel the need for a well-done look, there are many sauces and toppings suggested on pages 43-50. In time, with your own experimentation, you will undoubtedly create many new dishes.

Allow for STANDING time instead of serving food immediately

Remember that microwaves first touch the outer sections of food and then the center of the food. It will take a few minutes after the oven shuts off or the food is removed from the oven for the heat to disperse. This extra cooking time is called "standing time." Meats and poultry should be allowed to stand 10-15 minutes before making a final check for doneness. Similarly, in defrosting food, you will sometimes have to stir the food before allowing for standing time. Microwaves especially like water, fat, and sugar, so that if you are cooking, for example, a jelly-filled cupcake, it may feel cool to your touch but if you do not wait a few minutes for the heat to equalize, you may burn your tongue.

Think shape of containers and placement of food.

Sauces should be cooked in a deep dish or any large size measuring cup rather than in a dish with a flat surface. In the deep dish, microwaves penetrate the food more evenly than in a flat dish, where they will cook the food from the outer edges, leaving the center with little cooking unless it is stirred very often.

In arranging a dish or container in the oven, thin portions of food should be placed toward the center of the dish, with thicker portions toward the outside. When cooking more than one item, arrange items at least one inch apart. Never place food in the oven so that there is a circle of small items and one in the center. The food in the center will have a tendency to cook more slowly.

Your microwave oven will ease cooking for low-calorie diets and other special diets

The microwave oven eliminates the necessity of butter or oil to prevent pans from sticking and it utilizes different ways of cooking foods. Here are four easy ways:

1. Steam or poach food by covering and allowing it to cook in its own juices. Fish, chicken, vegetables, and fruits are delicious when cooked this way.

2. Stir-fry foods without adding any oil. There are recipes in this book for stir-frying chicken, beef, and vegetables.

3. Place meats and poultry with fat content on an inverted saucer in the bottom of the baking dish, or on a microwave rack or trivet so that the fat drips below.

4. Avoid sauces and toppings with high calories. Adapt existing recipes or create new ones that use sugar substitutes (lack of sugar will increase cooking time by 1 or 2 minutes), egg substitutes (which will not alter cooking time), herbs, and spices. Stretch, rather than heap, these sauces over foods.

Do not operate the oven when it is empty.

It is never necessary as in a conventional oven to preheat the oven. Always be sure food is in the microwave first. Then switch on the power.

DEFROSTING

In defrosting, the microwaves first come into contact with the outer portion of the frozen surface and the heat is then conducted toward the inner portion of the food. The Defrost setting automatically cycles these cooking periods at approximately 30% of power to prevent the surface from cooking before the inner portion is thawed.

Although most foods should be thawed on Defrost, there are some, such as poultry, frozen bread, cakes and pastries, small casseroles and foods with a lot of liquid that are defrosted on the Simmer setting and reduced to a setting of Defrost if the outside begins to cook.

In general, always under-defrost and let the food stand a little, or in the case of a food like hamburger, the defrosted part can be broken off, and frozen part put back in the oven. If foods begin to thaw unevenly, small pieces of aluminum foil may be used to reflect the microwaves away from the part that is beginning to cook faster. Cover the area with a small piece of foil and continue the defrosting procedure.

Frozen vegetables and pastries can be cooked on Full Power without defrosting them first. Fish can be partially thawed before cooking. Large cuts of meat and poultry should be completely thawed before they are cooked. It is best to remove them from the oven while they still feel cool and complete the thawing at room temperature. A microwave oven meat thermometer can tell you if the center is thawed. (40° F. after specified standing time.)

Steps in Defrosting:

1. Place frozen food in microwave oven.
2. Check defrosting charts for time required for thawing.
3. Set timer.
4. Set oven to Defrost Cycle and turn on oven.
5. Since most foods that are defrosting require periodic checks, you will need to open the door, thus interrupting the defrosting cycle, check the food, reposition it if necessary, reset the timer if additional time is required, and continue to defrost.

On the next page is a chart with times for defrosting poultry, meat and fish.

These times are for ovens with an automatic defrost cycle that works on 30 seconds, off 30 seconds intervals. (If your automatic defrost cycle works differently, you may need to adjust timings slightly.) For other foods, see Convenience Food Chart and Frozen Vegetable Table.

DEFROSTING CHART FOR POULTRY, MEAT and FISH

Food	Weight	Time	Procedure
Chicken Breasts	1 lb.	6 min.	1. Power on 3 min. Unwrap and separate. 2. Turn chicken skin-side-down. Power on 2 min. 3. Rearrange chicken breasts so that thawed portions are toward inside of dish and less thawed parts are toward outer edge. Power on 1 min. 4. Allow to stand several minutes.
Whole Chicken	3 lb.	12 min.	1. Power on 4 min. Unwrap. 2. Power on 3 min. Remove neck and giblets. 3. Power on 3 min. Turn chicken over. 4. Power on 2 min. 5. Allow standing time.
Whole Turkey	12 lb.	20 min. plus 20 min. plus 10 min. plus 10 min.	1. Power on 20 min. Unwrap. 2. Power on 20 min. Remove neck and giblets. 3. Power on 10 min. Turn turkey over. It may be necessary to cover tips of legs or wings with small pieces of aluminum foil. 4. Power on 6 min. Check and turn if necessary. 5. Power on 4 min. Allow standing time.
Turkey Parts	4 lb.	25 min.	1. Power on 10 min. Unwrap parts. 2. Power on 6 min. Turn over. 3. Power on 6 min. Check and turn if necessary. 4. Power on 4 min. It may be necessary to cover parts that start to cook with aluminum foil. 5. Power on 4 min. Allow standing time.
Duck or Goose	10 lb.	25 min. plus 24 min.	1. Power on 25 min. Unwrap. 2. Power on 12 min. Remove neck and giblets. Turn fowl over. 3. Power on 4 min. Check and turn if necessary. 4. Power on 4 min. Check and turn if necessary. 5. Power on 4 min. Allow standing time.
Cornish Games Hens (1 lb. each)	2 hens	16 min.	1. Power on 8 min. Unwrap. 2. Power on 4 min. Turn hens over. 3. Power on 4 min. Allow standing time.
Ground meat	1 lb.	6 min.	1. Power on 3 min. Unwrap and turn meat over. 2. Power on 2 min. Check and turn if necessary. 3. Power on 1 min. Allow standing time.
Chops	2 lb.	10 min.	1. Power on 6 min. Unwrap and separate. 2. Power on 2 min. Turn over. 3. Power on 2 min. Allow standing time.

Ribs	2 lb.	10 min.	1. Power on 6 min. Unwrap and separate. 2. Power on 2 min. Turn over. 3. Power on 2 min. Allow standing time.
Steaks	1 lb.	6 min.	1. Power on 4 min. Unwrap and separate. Turn over.
(3/4 in. thick)			2. Power on 2 min. Allow standing time.
Roasts	2 lb.	10 min.	1. Power on 4 min. Unwrap. 2. Power on 4 min. Turn roast over. 3. Power on 2 min. Allow standing time.

Fish and Seafood (may be cooked from frozen state)

			Hints for cooking
Fillets	1 lb.	3-1/2 min.	Separate 1/2 way through cooking
Whole Fish	12 oz.	1-1/2 min.	1. Cook in greased baking dish.
Lobster Tail	8-10 oz.	1-1/2 min.	2. Cook in shallow pie plate.
Shrimp	8-10 oz.	1-1/2 min.	3. Stir once during cooking.

BROWNING DISH

The empty browning dish must be preheated in the microwave oven; the surface temperature of the dish then becomes hot enough to sear and brown meats or other foods. After preheating the dish, the food is placed in the browning dish and returned to the microwave oven. The hot surface of the browning dish browns the food while the microwave power cooks the food. The food should be turned over halfway through the cooking time in order to brown on both sides.

Preheat time depends upon the type of food you wish to brown. Suggested preheat times are included with the browning dish. Preheat times vary from one minute for one fried egg to 5 to 6 minutes for steak. Follow manufacturers instructions for preheating.

The browning dish should not be used on conventional gas or electric range surface units, in the oven or under the broiler.

See the chart on the next page for using the browning dish.

Browning Dish Chart

Food	Quantity	Preheat Time on FULL POWER	Microwave Cooking Time
Steak	(1) 7 oz. 3/4-inch thick	3 to 5 min.	Cook uncovered 45 sec. Turn over and cook 1 min.
Steak, cubes	(1-2) 6-8 oz.	4 to 6 min. add 1 tsp. fat	Cook uncovered 45 sec. Turn over and cook 15 sec.
Hamburgers	1 or 2 patties	3 to 5 min.	Cook uncovered 1 min. Turn over and cook 1 min.
Pork Chops	1 or 2 chops 3/4 in. thick floured	4 to 5 min. add 1/2 tsp. fat after preheating.	Cook uncovered 5 min. Turn over after half of cooking time.
Chicken Pieces	(3 to 4 pieces) 8 to 12 oz. total, floured	4 to 6 min. Add 1 Tbs. fat after preheating.	Heat covered 7-9 min. Turn over after half of cooking time.
Fish Fillets	(2) 8 to 10 ozs. total, 1/4-inch thick, floured	4 to 6 min. 1 Tbs. fat after preheating.	Heat covered 3 min. Turn over after half of cooking time.
French Toast	(1 slice)	3 to 5 min. 1/2 tsp. fat after preheating	Heat uncovered 60 sec. Turn over after half of cooking time.
Grilled Cheese Sandwich	(1) outsides evenly but lightly buttered	3 to 5 min.	Heat uncovered 60 sec. Turn over after half of cooking time.
Eggs, Fried Sunny Side Up	(1 or 2) Puncture egg yolk first.	1 min. Add 1 Tbs. fat after preheating.	Heat covered 1 to 1-1/4 min.
Onions, Eggplant, and Rice	8 slices 4 slices 1 cup	3 to 5 min. Add 1 Tbs. fat after preheating	Heat uncovered 2 to 3 min. Turn over after half of cooking time.

HOW TO CONVERT YOUR FAVORITE RECIPE
FOR MICROWAVE COOKING

You can prepare almost any recipe in your microwave oven by making a few adjustments. Here's how you go about it.

If you can find a microwave recipe similar to the conventional one, use it as a guide. Most of the cooking methods called for can be done in the microwave oven. Follow the microwave recipe directions as to dish size, covering, techniques and timing.

In some cases, microwave cooking will produce different results which you may prefer. Since crusts don't form, omelets will not have a brown crust. This is an advantage in preparing souffles. They are less likely to fall, since they have no crust to shrink as they cool. Microwave cakes rise higher and are airier than their conventionally baked counterparts. They won't have a brown top, but can be frosted.

Points to keep in mind when you adapt your recipe:

*Moisture content

Microwaves cook food so rapidly that more moisture is retained, so less liquid or sauce is needed when preparing the recipe. Reduce the moisture content by at least 1/4. For example, a casserole may conventionally require one cup of water and one cup of soup. For microwave cooking, add one cup of soup, but reduce the water to three-quarters of a cup. This rule would not apply to dried vegetables and pasta, which need water to rehydrate.

*Seasoning

Use slightly less salt and strong flavorings. Adjustments to taste can be made after cooking.

*Timing

Your microwave oven will cook food in approximately 1/4 to 1/2 of the conventional time except for foods that need more time to rehydrate or tenderize.

*Power setting

For delicate liquids such as sweet or sour cream, cream or cottage cheese, and less tender cuts of meat, you should use a lower power setting (50% of power).

*Fat

Browning is frequently omitted, and fat is not needed to prevent sticking, so use just enough for flavor.

*Yeast breads

Dough needs more shortening to prevent toughness and dryness. Use about 1/4 cup shortening for 2-1/2 to 3 cups of flour.

Select recipes with whole grains for color, or those with toppings or frosting, since microwave oven breads do not brown. Of course, bread for sandwich loafs or canapes may be white and needs no crust. Similarly, bread for toasting may be white.

*Combining foods

Since pasta or dry vegetables take longer to cook than other ingredients in casseroles, you could substitute quick-cooking rice and canned beans. Quick-cooking rice is partially rehydrated, so double the amount of rice and reduce the liquid to obtain the same number of servings. Start cooking the uncooked pasta, and add remaining ingredients when it has become slightly tender.

Meat and vegetables for stews should be cut into smaller pieces to cook faster and more evenly.

*Cakes and Pies

Reduce liquid and leavening agents (such as baking powder and baking soda) by 1/4. For best results, beat the batter less than you would for conventional range baking and let it stand 10-15 minutes before baking to achieve a lighter texture and more even crust. Grease or line bottom *only* with wax paper (cut circle to fit bottom).

*Substitutions

The spices in any conventional recipe may be used in the microwave, and you can substitute freely.

Processed cheeses melt more smoothly and are easier to use than dry or hard natural cheeses. Open the oven as soon as the cheese softens and let the internal heat melt the cheese, or it will get tough and stringy.

If flour is substituted for cornstarch as the base of a sauce, it will thicken more slowly and need more stirring.

Use crushed croutons rather than bread crumbs for topping on casseroles. They give a drier, crisper surface. Sprinkle the crumbs on after the last stirring.

*Preventing sogginess

Appetizers, canapes and sandwiches should be wrapped in a paper napkin or placed on a paper towel lined plate before being heated. The paper absorbs the moisture from steam trapped between the food and the plate.

*Changing the yield

Once you have converted a recipe, you may wish to make a change in quantity. If you double the recipe it will take 1/2 to 2/3 more time to cook. Select a container that will keep the depth of the ingredients the same no matter whether the recipe is doubled or halved. A smaller amount spread thinner in a large dish will cook faster and less evenly. A larger amount in too small a bowl may boil over.

Below is an example of the way one recipe was converted:

Chicken Cacciatore

2 Tbsp. margarine
3 lb. broiler-fryer, cut up
1 onion, sliced
1 green pepper, sliced
1 garlic clove, minced
1 (16 oz.) can tomatoes
1 tsp. salt
1 tsp. sugar
1/4 tsp. each, pepper,
    ground allspice
1 bay leaf
dash hot pepper sauce

Preheat oven to 375°. Melt margarine in 10-inch skillet over moderate heat; add chicken pieces and brown well on all sides; remove to 2 qt. casserole. To skillet drippings add the sliced onion, green pepper and garlic; cook until onion is soft. Chop tomatoes and add to skillet. Stir in salt, sugar, pepper, ground allspice, bay leaf and hot pepper sauce. Heat to boiling then pour over chicken in casserole and bake in oven about 45 minutes until chicken is tender. 4 servings

To convert the recipe:

1. In a 2-quart casserole or baking dish place margarine, onion, green pepper and garlic. Microwave on FULL POWER 5 minutes or until just tender.

2. Drain tomatoes; reserve juice. Cut up tomatoes.

3. Add tomatoes and seasonings to onion mixture.

4. Arrange chicken pieces in the sauce with meatiest portion toward outside of dish. Turn pieces to coat with sauce.

5. Cover with lid or plastic wrap. Microwave on FULL POWER 10 minutes.

6. Stir; recover; continue to cook on FULL POWER 10 to 15 minutes or until fork tender.

7. If sauce is too thick add some reserved tomato juice.

Microwave time: 25-30 mins.
Conventional range time: 60 mins.

KITCHEN-METRICS

Within the next ten years, the United States will converting to metric measurement. A dual measuring cup is available now that has a capacity of 250 milliliters for measuring liquids. On one side it is graduated in quarters. On the other side it is graduated in measurements of 50, 100, 150, 200, and 250.

A set of 4 measuring spoons would be:
(approximate measure)
1 tablespoon = 15 milliliters
1 teaspoon = 5 milliliters
1/2 teaspoon = 2.5 milliliters
1/4 teaspoon = 1.25 milliliters

Metric weight and avoirdupois equivalents are:
(approximate measure)
1 ounce = 28-1/2 grams
1 pound = 450 grams = 1/2 kilogram
1 kilogram = 2.20 pounds = 1000 grams

Dry Measure Volume Equivalents

Dry measure is used for fresh fruits and vegetables when measuring rather large quantities.

1 quart = 2 pints = 1.1 liters
8 quarts = 1 peck = 8.8 liters
4 pecks = 1 bushel = 35 liters

Dry measure is expressed in grams and kilograms.

Temperatures are expressed in Celsius. For example, for a baking temperature of 325° F., the equivalent is 163° C.

In this book abbreviations in the recipes
will be used as follows.
Tablespoon = Tbs.
teaspoon = tsp.
ounce = oz.
pound = lb.

Gram = g
liter = l
kilogram = k

Temperatures refer to degrees Farenheit.

Convenience Foods

CHAPTER 2

CONVENIENCE FOOD CHART

As microwave cooking gains in popularity more manufacturers are putting microwave instructions on packages and changing to paper board trays instead of foil.

Some of these prebreaded products will become very moist in the microwave oven. Although laying them out on a paper towel while heating may help, do not expect them to be crispy. They do, however, reheat well.

Product	Weight	Directions	Microwave Time
Appetizers			
Frozen Mixed Appetizers	6 ozs.	Arrange in circle on paper towel or plate	1 min., 15 secs.
Cholesterol-Free Artificial Bacon Strips	5-1/4 ozs.	Arrange on paper towel with plate underneath. Cover with paper towel.	1-1/2 min.
Cholesterol-Free Artificial Link Sausages	8 ozs.	Arrange in circle on paper towel Cover with paper towel	2 min.
Cholesterol-Free Artificial Sausage Patties	8-ozs.	Arrange in circle on paper towel Cover with paper towel.	2 min.
Frozen Crab Puffs	7 ozs.	Arrange in circle on paper towel	1 min.
Frozen Egg Rolls	6 ozs.	Arrange in circle on paper towel	1 min. 15 secs.
Frozen Pieroges	8 ozs.	Arrange in circle on paper towel	2 min.
Frozen Pizza Rolls	6 ozs.	Arrange in circle on paper towel	2 min.
Frozen Beef Taquitos	11-1/2 ozs.	Arrange in circle on paper towel or towel..	4-5 min.
Frozen Cocktail Tacos	5-1/2 ozs.	Arrange in circle on paper towel or towel.	4-5 min.
Tortillas, Corn	14 ozs.	Slit package. Place on dish.	3-5 min.
Tortillas, Flour	12-1/2 ozs.	Slit package. Place on dish.	3-5 min.
Beverages			
Cocoa Mix	1 cup	Fill cup with water. Heat. Stir in cocoa mix.	1-1/4 min. Stir.
Instant Coffee or Tea	1 cup	Fill cup with cold water. Heat. Stir in coffee or tea.	2-1/4-2-1/2 min. Stir.
Frozen Non-Dairy Creamer	1 pint carton	Place in oven.	3 min. Shake often.
Frozen Juices	6 oz. can	Remove top. Heat to loosen; empty into pitcher. Heat to soften.	15 sec. in can. 15 sec. in pitcher.

Product	Weight	Directions	Microwave Time
Soups			
Canned Soups	10-1/2 ozs.	Pour soup in bowl. Add water as directed on can.	3-4 min.
Dehydrated Soup Mix	1 envelope	Pour into 2-3 bowls. Combine with liquid in each bowl.	2-3 min. Stir twice.
Frozen Soups	10 ozs.	Pour in bowl. Add liquid as directed.	5-6 min. Stir.
Frozen Won-Ton Soup	15 ozs.	Pour in bowl. Add liquid as directed.	6-7 min. Stir.
Sandwiches			
Frozen English Muffin Halves with Ham and Cheese Topping	10 ozs. 4 halves	Arrange on paper plate uncovered.	3-1/2-4 min.
Frozen Corn Dogs	12-1/2 ozs.	Arrange on paper plate uncovered.	2-1/4 min.
Frozen Reuben Sandwiches	9 ozs. 2 sand-wiches	Remove plastic covering. Place on 2 plates	2-1/2 min.
Main Courses			
Frozen Dinners-Entrees (Meat and Potato)	9-9-1/2 ozs.	Remove foil cover from foil tray and return to paper carton or cover tray with wax paper.	6-7 min.
Frozen 2-3 Course Dinner	15-16 ozs.	Remove foil cover from foil tray and return tray to paper carton or cover tray with wax paper.	7-8 min.
Frozen Foreign Dinners	10 ozs.	Remove foil cover from foil tray and return tray to paper carton or cover tray with wax paper.	6 min.
Frozen Low Calorie Dinners	16 ozs.	Remove foil cover from foil tray and return tray to paper carton or cover tray with wax paper.	8 min.
Frozen Breakfasts	4-1/2 ozs.	Remove foil cover from foil tray and return tray to paper carton or cover with wax paper.	2-1/2-3 min. (French toast and pancakes cook in minimum time.)
Canned Casserole Mixture	8 oz. can (1 cup)	Put on dinner plate and cover with lid or plastic wrap.	1-1/2 min.
Canned Casserole Mixture	16 oz. can (2 cups)	Empty into casserole.	2-1/2 min. Stir once.
Canned Casserole Mixture	24 ozs. (3 cups)	Empty into casserole.	4 min. Stir once.
Canned Casserole Mixture	40 ozs. (5 cups)	Empty into casserole.	7 min. Stir once.
Casserole "Helpers" (with freeze-dried meats)	6-1/2 ozs.	Brown meat in browning dish; then combine mix with additions on package directions.	4-5 min. 8-9 min. Stir; let stand 5 min.

Product	Weight	Directions	Microwave Time
Main Courses (cont.)			
Casserole "Helpers" (you add ground beef)	3-1/2 ozs.	Crumble ground beef and sprinkle with seasoning from mix Add other ingredients. Reduce liquid by 1/4 cup.	3-5 min. 1/2 lb. to 1 lb. Stir.
Skillet Casserole Mixes (you add ground beef)	12-18 ozs.	Crumble ground beef and sprinkle with seasoning from mix Add other ingredients. Reduce liquid by 1/4 cup.	1 lb. meat 5-7 min. Stir.
Fish			
Frozen Clam Cakes	7 ozs.	Place in bowl.	4-5 min.
Frozen Clam Pie	7ozs.	Remove from foil. Put in bowl.	4-6 min.
Frozen Fried Clams	5 ozs.	Place on paper towel. Rearrange after first 30 seconds.	1 min.
Frozen Crabmeat or Lobster Meat	6 ozs.	Place in bowl.	30 secs. -1 min.
Frozen Precooked and Breaded Fish Sticks	8 ozs.	Arrange in circle on paper plate.	3 min.
Frozen Precooked and Breaded Fish, Scallops, or Shrimp	7 ozs.	Arrange in circle on paper plate.	1-1/2 min.
Frozen Fish with Sauce	11 ozs.	Leave in foil tray with cooking film cover.	8 min. rearrange package once.
Frozen Fish without Sauce	10 ozs.	Place on platter and cover.	7 min. turn once.
Cod, Haddock, Perch Pollack, Trout	11-1/2 ozs.	Place on platter and cover.	8 min. Turn once.
	16 ozs.	Place on platter and cover.	9-10 min. Turn once.
Frozen Lobster Newburg	10 ozs.	Slit pouch. Turn twice.	4-5 min.
Frozen Oysters	7 ozs.	Arrange in circle on a paper towel.	30 secs.
Frozen Tuna Pie	8 ozs.	Remove from foil. Place in bowl	5-7 min.
Meat and Poultry			
Frozen Green Chili Burritos	12 ozs.	Place on paper towel.	5-7 min. uncovered.
Frozen, Creamed, Chipped Beef	14 ozs.	Place in container covered with wax paper.	6-7 min.
Frozen Beef Enchiladas	32 ozs.	Remove from foil container. Cook in covered container.	12-14 min.
Frozen Roast Beef Hash	11-1/2 ozs.	Place uncovered in glass dish.	6-1/2-6-3/4 min.; stir once
Frozen Stuffed Cabbage Rolls	14 ozs.	Remove from foil container. Place in covered casserole.	8 mins.; stir once.

Product	Weight	Directions	Microwave Time
Meat and Poultry (cont.)			
Frozen Battered and Cooked chicken	17-1/4 ozs.	Arrange on place with meatier sides toward edges.	6 min.; stir once.
Frozen Creamed Chicken or Turkey	6-1/2 ozs.	Place in covered casserole.	5-6 mins.; stir twice.
Frozen Escalloped Chicken and Noodles	12 ozs.	Place uncovered in a casserole.	8-10 min.
Frozen Chicken and Onions and Gravy	1/4 lb. of a 3 lb. chicken	Place in a covered dish.	8-10 min.
Frozen Chicken or Turkey Pie	8-10 ozs.	Remove from foil container. Place in same size bowl. Cover.	6-8 min.
Hamburger Patties, Cooked	4 ozs.	Place uncovered in a dish.	1-1/4-1-1/2 min.
Frozen Macaroni, Beef and Tomatoes	11-1/2 ozs.	Remove from foil container. Place in covered casserole.	7-8 min.; stir twice.
Frozen Lasagna with Cheese and Meat	12 ozs.	Remove from foil. Place in covered casserole.	7-1/2-8-1/2 min.; stir twice.
Frozen Meat Loaf	1-1/2 lbs.	Place in loaf dish. Cover with wax paper.	**Defrost** 9 min. **Cook** 10-12 min. more.
Frozen Meat Pie	8-10 ozs.	Remove from foil container. Place in glass dish of same size.	7-1/2 min.
Frozen Green Peppers with Beef	14 ozs.	Remove from foil. Cook in covered casserole.	6-8 min.
Sweet and Sour Pork	14 ozs.	Remove from foil container. Place in serving dish and cover.	7-9 min.
Green Pepper Steak with Rice	10-1/2 ozs.	Remove from foil container. Place in covered casserole.	5-7 min.
Veal Parmigiana	32 ozs.	Remove from foil container. Place in 3-qt. container.	12-14 min.
Frozen Rabbit	2-1/4 lbs.	Arrange pieces on platter. Cover.	**Defrost** 3-5 min.; turn. **Cook** 5-6 min.
Frozen Cooked Barbecued Ribs	2 lbs.	**Defrost** in plastic carton. Then transfer to platter. Cover.	**Defrost** 2-4 min. transfer. **Cook** 4-5 min.
Frozen Shortribs of Beef	11-1/2 ozs.	Place in covered casserole.	9-10 min. stir twice.
Vienna Sausages	5 oz. can	Arrange on plate.	45 secs.
Frozen Sloppy Joe Sauce with Beef	26 ozs.	Remove from foil. Place in covered 2-qt. casserole.	9-10 mins.; stir twice.
Frozen Turkey Roast	32 ozs.	Remove from foil container. Place in covered casserole.	30 mins.
Frozen Turkey Tetrazzini	12 ozs.	Remove from foil container. Place in covered casserole.	6-8 min.; stir twice.

Product	Weight	Directions	Microwave Time
Eggs and Cheese			
Frozen Cheese Ravioli in Tomato Sauce	12-1/2 ozs.	Remove from foil container. Cook in covered container.	5-6 min.; stir once.
Egg Beaters	8 ozs.	Place carton in microwave oven	1 min.; stir once.
Macaroni and Cheese Sauce Mix	7-1/4 ozs.	Combine all ingredients in covered casserole.	10 min.; stir.
Frozen Macaroni and Cheese	12 ozs.	Remove from foil container. Cook in covered casserole.	7-8 min.; stir twice.
Frozen Quiche Lorraine	22 ozs.	Remove from foil container. Place in glass pie plate.	18 min. at 30% of power.
Frozen Welsh Rarebit	10 ozs.	Remove from foil container. Cook in covered casserole.	7-8 min.; stir twice.
Vegetables			
Frozen French Fries	16 ozs.	Place on paper plate (will not turn golden brown.)	5-6 min.
Frozen Baked Stuffed Potatoes	2 med. 12 ozs.	Heat uncovered on plate.	3-1/4-3-1/2 min.
Mashed Potato Flakes	1-1/2 cups	Follow package directions, heating milk and butter and adding to Flakes in a covered casserole.	2-3 min.
Scalloped Potato Mix	5-1/8 ozs.	Combine ingredients in covered casserole according to directions on package.	14-16 min.; stir.
Frozen Taters	16 ozs.	Place on paper towel on paper plate (will not turn golden brown).	5-6 min.
Frozen Eggplant Parmigiana	12 ozs.	Remove from tin. Place in covered bowl.	4-6 min.
Frozen Fried Onion Rings	16 ozs. 30-32 rings	Place in shallow dish and cover with wax paper.	3-1/2-4 min. for 16 rings.
Frozen Rice and Vegetables	7 ozs.	Place in covered casserole or bowl.	3-4 min.; stir once.
Frozen Vegetables: See pages		for cooking other fresh and frozen vegetables.	
Canned Vegetables	8 oz.	Place in covered casserole or bowl. Drain most liquid.	1-1/2-2 min.
Canned Vegetables	12 oz. can	Place in covered casserole or bowl. Drain most liquid.	2-1/2 min.
Breads and Pastries			
Frozen Baking Powder Biscuits	2 biscuits 4 biscuits 6 biscuits	Place on napkin or plate	30-40 sec. 45-55 sec. 60-75 sec.
Frozen Bread	4 slices	Arrange on paper towel.	15-30 sec.

Product	Weight	Directions	Microwave Time
Breads and Pastries (cont.)			
Frozen Rolls precooked and browned	2 rolls 4 rolls 6 rolls	Heat uncovered on paper towel or plate.	15-30 sec. 45-60 sec. 60-75 sec.
Frozen Brownies (frosted)	13 ozs.	Remove from foil container. Place in glass dish.	1-2 min.
Frozen Cheese Cake	17 ozs.	Remove from foil Place on plate.	**Defrost** 1 min.
Frozen Cheese Cake	1 serv.	Place on plate.	30 sec.
Frozen Corn Muffin Batter	10 oz. pkg.	To defrost: remove from wrappings. Place in covered bowl.	**Defrost** 1 min.; **Cook** 1-2 min.
Frozen Coffee Cake	11 ozs.	Remove from foil container. Cook on serving plate uncovered.	1-1/2-2-1/2 min.
Frozen Cake without Frosting	1 slice	Place on paper napkin.	15 sec.
Frozen Layer Cake with Frosting	17 ozs.	Remove from paper container. and place on dish.	1-2 min.
Frozen Cinnamon Rolls, Danish Pastry, Sweet Rolls	2 servings	Cook uncovered on paper towel or serving dish.	1-1/2-2 min.
Frozen Doughnuts	2 med.	Cook uncovered on paper towel or dish.	40-45 sec. Let stand 2 min.
Apple Dumplings	2 med. servs.	Place in dish.	5-5-1/2 min. Let stand 5 min.
Apple Pandowdy	15 ozs.	Remove from foil. Place in dish.	12-15 min.
Frozen Creamed Pies	8 or 9" pie	Remove from foil pan and place on glass plate.	10-15 sec.
Frozen Cooked Fruit Pies	9" pie	Remove from foil pan and place on glass plate.	3-5 min.
Frozen Pancake Batter	10 oz. pkg.	To defrost: open paper container on one end.	1-1/2-2 min.
Frozen Uncooked Pie Shell	9"	To defrost: remove from foil. Place in glass. Prick with fork tines.	**Defrost** 1-2 min.
Frozen Waffles	1 section	Place on paper towel or plate.	30 sec.
Desserts			
Apple and Cherry Blintzes	15 ozs.	Place on paper towel. Arrange in circle.	8-10 min. uncovered; turn once.
Peach Cobbler	32 ozs.	Remove from foil container. Place in bowl.	25 min.
Custard Mix and Pudding Mix	3 ozs.	Follow directions on package in 4 cups measuring cup, uncovered.	5 min.; stir.

Product	Weight	Directions	Microwave Time
Desserts (cont.)			
Danish Dessert	4 ozs.	Add 2 cups of water to mix in large bowl.	5 min.; stir.
Frozen Pudding	17-1/2 ozs.	Cook in plastic carton, covered.	1-1/2 min.; stir twice.
Frozen Fruit	10 ozs.	Place in serving dish.	**Defrost** 1 min.; then **Cook** 30 sec.
Ice Cream Topping	1/2 cup	Remove metal lid. Heat jar.	45 sec.; stir once.
Frozen Whipped Topping	4-1/2 ozs.	Remove cover and heat in plastic container.	10 sec.; stir twice.
Sauces			
Frozen Sauces	8 ozs.	Remove from foil pouch. Place in bowl. Cover.	2-1/2-3-1/2 min. Stir twice.
Canned Sauces	8 oz. can	Place in bowl. Cover.	1-3/4 min.; stir twice.
Gravy Mix	5/8 oz. pkg.	Follow package directions. Place in bowl. Cover.	2 min.; stir
Hollandaise Sauce Mix	5/8 oz. pkg.	Follow package directions. Place in bowl.	2-1/2 min.; stir often.
Other			
Butter, Melting	1-4 Tbs. 1/4-1/2 cup 1/2-1 cup	Place in plastic or glass	15 sec. 30 sec. 45 sec.
Frozen Pasta (Cavatelli, Gnocchi, Tortellini)	16 ozs.	Place in container filled with warm water, according to package directions.	10-13 min. Let stand.
Pizza	8"	Place in browning dish.	8 min.

REHEATING FOODS

These reheat times are to be considered guidelines since the time can vary according to type, quantity, and temperature of food and container. To reheat foods at **refrigerator temperature**, increase heating time by 50%. For reheating foods at room temperature:

Beverages and Liquids: Heat uncovered, 1-2 min. per mug.

Breads and Cakes: Reheat on a paper napkin, cloth napkin, or paper plate

> Bagels and Plain Doughnuts: 10 secs. for first one; 5 secs. for each additional one.

> Bread Slices, Dinner or Sweet Rolls, and Toaster Pastries: 5 secs. per piece.

Casseroles, Rice, Noodles, Soups, Vegetables: Cover bowl or plate with ceramic lid, plastic wrap or wax paper (but not a paper towel which will not keep moisture within the food). One min. per cup.

Dinner Plate (Meat or Fish, Potato and Vegetable): Cover bowl or plate and use minimum time for fish and maximum for meat. Add 1/2 tsp. (2-1/2 ml) of water to fish so it won't be dry.

> 1 plate   50 sec. to 1 min.
> 2 plates   1-1/2 to 2 min.

Eggs (Poached, Fried, Scrambled): Cover and do not overcook or they will tend to become rubbery. 30 secs. for first egg; 15 secs. for each additional egg.

Fish, Shellfish, Meats and Poultry: (Add 1/2 tsp. or 2-1/2 ml of water over each serving of fish.) Cover with plastic wrap. Do not overcook. 1/2 min. per slice.

Pies: Heat 9″ pie 3 min. 1 wedge: 15 sec.

Rice and Noodles: Cover and stir once during cooking. 1 min. per cup.

Sandwiches: Wrap in wax paper or paper napkin. 1(5-oz.), 45 sec. to 1 min. 2(5-oz.) each, 1-1/2 min.

Vegetables: Cover and stir once during cooking. Heat 1 min. per cup.

Your First 100 Minutes of Microwave Cooking

CHAPTER 3

MEAL PREPARATION

Sequence of preparation is important when you plan to serve several foods from the oven at the same meal. Foods vary in the way in which they hold heat. Usually those that heat the slowest lose heat less quickly, and those that heat the fastest, lose heat more quickly. By planning the preparation sequence, all foods can be ready to serve at the same time. Even an unexpected interruption will not disrupt your plans because foods are easy to reheat.

Consider the following in your preparation sequence:
1) How long is the cooking time?
2) What is the optimum serving temperature?
3) How long will the food hold the heat?
4) Is there a covering to hold in the heat?
5) Can the cooking time be broken into segments?

Here are some basic guidelines for preparation of a meal:
1) **Dessert items, unless served hot, are usually prepared first and allowed to cool while the rest of the meal is being prepared.**
2) **Meat and casserole items usually have the most flexibility. They hold heat well, can be reheated and can have their cooking time broken into two or three segments. The exceptions are eggs, cheese, and fish which cook so rapidly that they should be cooked shortly before serving.**
3) **Vegetables have limited flexibility. They can be reheated, but some may become overcooked if they stand too long.**
4) **Breads are usually the last items in the oven. They do not hold the heat well and may become dry with reheating.**
5) **Consult Reheating Foods Chart on page 29.**

The following menus have something for everybody. Pick, mix and match recipes that suit your family's taste. Note how many foods that used to be a weekend treat can now be enjoyed any time because of the ease of preparation and minimum cooking time by microwaves.

Undercook at the beginning and plan ahead.

BEVERAGES

Beverage Heating Times in microwave oven:

1 cup (1/4 l) . . . . .2 min.
2 cups (1/2 l) . . . . .3-3-1/2 min.

Instant Coffee

3/4 cup (1/6 l) cold water

1. Pour water into a heat-resistant, non-metallic mug or cup.
2. Heat at FULL POWER uncovered in microwave oven 1 to 2 minutes.
3. Add desired amount of instant coffee. Stir.

Hot Cocoa

3 Tbs.	unsweetened cocoa	45 ml
1/4 cup	sugar	1/16 l
1/4 cup	cold water	1/16 l
3 cups	milk	3/4 l

1. Combine cocoa, sugar, and water in a heat-resistant, non-metallic pitcher or in individual serving mugs or cups.
2. Heat at FULL POWER uncovered in microwave oven 2 minutes.
3. Stir in milk and heat, uncovered, in microwave oven 4-1/2 to 5-1/2 minutes or until hot. Do not allow milk to boil.

Serves 4.

Tea

3/4 cup	cold water	1/6 l
(1 tea bag or)	tea (in tea ball)	5 ml
1 tsp.		

1. Pour water into a heat-resistant, non-metallic mug or cup.
2. Heat at FULL POWER uncovered in microwave oven 1-1/2 to 2-1/2 minutes.
3. Submerge tea bag (or tea ball) in water.
4. Allow to steep 1 to 2 minutes or until desired strength is reached.

Mulled Fruit Drink

1 quart	A combination of any of the following: cider; cranberry, apple, raspberry, pineapple, and orange juice; tea	1 l
2-3	whole cloves	
12"	cinnamon stick	
1/4 cup	brown sugar	1/16 l
1/2	orange, thinly sliced	
1/2	lemon, thinly sliced	

1. Place all the ingredients in a 2-quart container. Cover with wax paper.
2. Place in microwave oven. Cook at FULL POWER 8-10 minutes; stir once.
3. Store in refrigerator to reheat, according to Reheating Foods Chart, when desired.

Serves 4-8.

Microwave time: 8-10 minutes
Conventional range time: 20-30 minutes

BREAKFAST SUGGESTIONS

Scrambled Eggs

1 tsp.	butter per egg	5 ml
1 Tbs.	light cream or milk	15 ml
number desired	eggs	
to taste	pepper	

1. Melt butter in a small 1 qt. bowl for 15 to 45 seconds, depending on amount.
2. Beat remaining ingredients (use an egg beater) until well blended in another bowl. Pour into butter.
3. Cover and cook at FULL POWER as follows: 30 to 45 seconds per egg. Stir occasionally.
4. Allow eggs to stand 1 to 2 minutes prior to serving.

Omelet

2	eggs	
2 Tbs.	milk or light cream	30 ml
1/8 tsp.	salt	5/8 ml
to taste	pepper	
2 tsp.	butter or margarine	10 ml
pinch	tarragon or thyme	

1. In a small 1 qt. bowl beat eggs, milk, salt and pepper. (Use an egg beater.)
2. In a cereal or soup bowl melt butter for 15 seconds.
3. Pour egg mixture into bowl and cover tightly with plastic wrap.
4. Cook at FULL POWER in microwave oven for 45 seconds.
5. With a rubber spatula or fork, move cooked eggs toward center.
6. Cook at FULL POWER covered, in microwave oven for 1 minute.
7. Let stand, covered, at least 1-1/2 minutes.
8. Loosen egg from dish with a rubber spatula. (If omelet is not cooked enough, return omelet to oven for an additional 30 seconds.)

Variations:

Cheese Omelet: Sprinkle omelet with 1/4 cup (1/16 liter) shredded cheese after Step 6. Cover and return to microwave oven for an additional 30 seconds to melt cheese. Continue with Step 7.

Bacon Omelet: Crumble bacon into egg mixture during Step 1. If desired, some of the bacon drippings may be used in place of the butter.

Mushroom Omelet: When melting butter in Step 2, saute 1/4 cup (1/16 liter) mushrooms. Cooking time is 2 minutes.

Serves 1.

Bacon

Arrange two to three layers of paper toweling on a paper plate. Arrange separated slices of bacon on the plate. Cover with paper toweling. (If layering bacon, separate each layer with paper toweling.)

Cook at FULL POWER as follows: 1 to 1-1/2 min. per slice.

Cooking times vary with bacon depending on the thickness, brand, starting temperature, and degree of doneness desired. Bacon becomes crisp during the standing time allowed before serving.

Toast

Prepare in toaster. If it needs reheating, place toast in a single layer on paper toweling and heat in microwave oven at FULL POWER as follows: 15 to 30 seconds per slice.

Regular Oatmeal

1-1/2 cups	regular oatmeal	3/8 l
3 cups	water (room temperature)	3/4 l
3/4 tsp.	salt	3-3/4 ml

1. Measure oatmeal in a 2-quart, heat-resistant, non-metallic casserole.
2. Add room temperature water and salt. Stir well.
3. Cook at FULL POWER, uncovered, in microwave oven 4 minutes. Stir again.
4. Heat at FULL POWER 4 minutes longer. Stir well, cover, and let stand about 4 minutes per serving.

Serves 4 to 6.

Coffee Cake Mix (any flavor)

Prepare cake mix according to directions on the package. Pour batter into an ungreased round bundt-type pan. If you do not have such a pan, place a glass, about 2 inches in diameter, in the center of an ungreased 8 or 9 inch round cake dish or bowl. Let stand 10 minutes before putting in oven.

Cook at FULL POWER 6 minutes or until top is *almost* dry. Let stand 10 minutes. Twist glass and remove if you have created your own bundt pan.

NOTE: For microwave ovens with variable controls, prepare cake mix as directed except set oven control to SIMMER (50% power). Cook at FULL POWER 6 minutes. Then cook at FULL POWER 3 to 4 minutes or until top is almost dry. Let stand 10 minutes. Twist glass and remove.

Serves 6 to 8

Microwave time: 6 to 10 minutes
Conventional range time: 25 to 30 minutes at 325°

Muffins

1. Prepare mix according to package directions.
2. Cook at FULL POWER in plastic coffee cup holders or 6 ounce custard cups lined with muffin papers. (Fill each cup halfway.) Muffin pans for microwave ovens are also available.

Allow 30 seconds per muffin.

APPETIZERS

Low-Cal Crunchies

Great low-cal crunchies for cocktail accompaniment can be made from nuts, seeds, frozen beans, and green peas. Crunch limas are a favorite in China.

1. Defrost 1 package frozen lima beans and/or peas or substitute 2 cups nuts or seeds.
2. Spread on paper towel or shallow plate and cook at FULL POWER in microwave oven 6 minutes.
3. Make coating of:

1/4 cup	salad or cooking oil	1/16 l
1 Tbs.	soy, teriyaki or Worcestershire sauce	15 ml
1 tsp.	seasoning salt	5 ml
1 tsp.	sodium glutamate (optional)	5 ml

Mix all together thoroughly.

4. Coat vegetables, seeds, or nuts in above sauce.
5. Spread on shallow pan and cook at FULL POWER in microwave oven for 6 minutes.
7. Spread on paper towel to dry.
8. When cool, store in tight container.

Microwave time: 6 minutes
Conventional range time: 15-25 minutes at 425°

Stuffed Mushrooms

16 to 20 mushrooms, medium to large caps

3 Tbs.	butter, melted	45 ml
1/4 cup	onion, minced	1/16 l
1/2 cup	parsley, minced	1/8 l
1/2 cup	dry bread crumbs	1/8 l
	salt, pepper,	
	nutmeg, paprika	
1/2 cup	cooked or canned chicken	1/8 l
	or veal, minced	
1/2 cup	bechamel sauce	1/8 l
	(see page 46)	
1/4 cup	Romano or Parmesan	1/16 l
	cheese, grated	

1. Clean mushrooms; remove stems and chop them.
2. Place butter in a large, flat casserole in microwave oven and cook at FULL POWER 30 seconds.
3. Add mushroom caps. Heat at FULL POWER 1 minute, then turn and cook at FULL POWER 1 minute more.
4. Remove mushrooms and in remaining juices, add onion and cook at FULL POWER 1 minute or until it is soft.
5. Remove pan from oven. Stir in chopped mushrooms, bread crumbs, seasoning, chicken or veal, and bechamel sauce.
6. Fill mushroom caps and sprinkle with cheese.
7. Refrigerate until ready for use, or place in microwave oven 4-6 minutes or until cheese has just melted.
8. Remove and sprinkle with more paprika and parsley.

Serves 8-10 people.

Microwave time: 7-1/2 to 9-1/2 minutes
Conventional range time: 20 minutes at 375°

SNACKS

Here is a guide to cook some popular snacks. All times are for foods at room temperature.

Frankfurters or Hot Dogs

Directions: Place hot dog in a hot dog bun. Wrap in a paper napkin.

Time: Cook for 1/2 minute per hot dog

Hamburger Guide

Directions: Hamburgers should be cooked first and then put into a bun. If you want to brown hamburgers, follow directions on Browning Dish Chart on page 16. Otherwise, place hamburgers in a shallow rectangular container and cover loosely with wax paper. Turn after first 1-1/2 minutes. One pound of hamburger makes 4-6 patties depending on thickness and size.

Time: Cook 1-1/2 to 2-1/2 minutes per patty.

Cheese Savories

1/2 cup	butter	1/8 l
1-1/2 cups	flour	1/3 l
1/2 lb.	sharp Cheddar cheese, shredded	260 g
1 tsp.	salt	5 ml
1/2 tsp.	paprika	2-1/2 ml

1. Combine all ingredients, cutting butter into flour and cheese mixture with a pastry blender.
2. Form into balls the size of walnuts.
3. Chill for several hours or overnight in refrigerator or freeze for future use.
4. Place 6-8 savories on a large, greased, heat-resistant dish in microwave oven and heat at FULL POWER 4-6 minutes. (If frozen, heat at FULL POWER 6-8 minutes.)
5. Do not overcook. The high cheese content will continue cooking during standing time.
6. While hot, sprinkle with paprika and serve warm.

Makes 25-30 savories.

Conventional range time: 10-15 minutes at 425°

DINNER FOR FOUR

Here is a sample dinner menu to use in your first 100 minutes of microwave cooking.

New England Clam Chowder
Meat Loaf   Baked Potatoes
Crunchy Green Beans
Baked Apple

Instructions for sample menu:

1. Prepare and cook baked apples. Set aside with covering of plastic wrap to keep warm. If you prefer cold apples, refrigerate them.
2. Prepare and cook chowder. Set aside and reheat later.
3. Prepare meat loaf through step 2.
4. Cook potatoes. Set aside wrapped in foil to keep warm.
5. Prepare and cook green beans. Set aside covered.
6. Cook meat loaf according to steps 3, 4, and 5.
7. Reheat soup.
8. Reheat beans if necessary for 45 seconds.
9. Enjoy your dinner!

Baked Apples

4 large Cortland baking apples or Rome beauties

4 tsp.	brown sugar	20 ml
4 tsp.	butter or margarine	20 ml
4-1/2 tsp.	nutmeg	10 ml
4-1/2 tsp.	cinnamon	10 ml
1/2 cup	currants	1/8 l

1. Wash and core apples. Peel an inch of peel from the stem end of the apples.
2. Place apples in non-metallic baking dish.
3. Fill each apple with ingredients.
4. Cook at FULL POWER for 7 minutes, or until the apples are tender.

Serves 4.

Microwave time: 8-10 minutes
Conventional range time: 40-60 minutes at 350°

Variations: Other fillings may be used, such as chutney sauce, cranberry sauce, marshmallows, raisins, blanched almonds, currant jelly, and marzipan.

New England Clam Chowder

3 slices	raw bacon	
1 8-oz. can	minced clams, undrained	240 g
1-1/2 cups	peeled and cubed potatoes	3/8 l
1/3 cup	finely chopped onion	1/12 l
2 Tbs.	flour	30 ml
1-1/2 cups	milk	3/8 l
1 cup	light cream or canned milk, undiluted	1/4 l
1 tsp.	salt	5 ml
1/2 tsp.	pepper	5/8 ml
1/4 tsp.	fresh chopped chives	1-1/4 ml
3 Tbs.	sherry	45 ml

1. Place bacon in a deep, 2-qt., heat-resistant, non-metallic casserole.
2. Cook at FULL POWER, covered with a paper towel, in microwave oven 4 minutes or until bacon is crisp.
3. Remove cooked bacon with a slotted spoon. Crumble bacon and set aside. Reserve drippings in casserole.
4. Drain liquid from clams and add liquid to bacon drippings. Set clams aside.
5. Add potatoes and onion to casserole.
6. Cook at FULL POWER covered in microwave oven 8 minutes or until vegetables are tender; stir occasionally.
7. Blend flour into vegetable mixture.
8. Gradually stir in milk until smooth.
9. Cook at FULL POWER, uncovered, in microwave oven 4 minutes or until thickened and smooth.
10. Stir in cream, salt, pepper, and reserved clams, and sherry.
11. Cook at FULL POWER, uncovered, in microwave oven 4 minutes or until heated through. Garnish with crumbled bacon and chives before serving.

Serves 4-6.

Meat Loaf

1-1/2 lbs.	ground beef	68 g
1	egg	
1 slice	fresh bread, crumbled	
1 small	onion, chopped or	
1 Tbs.	instant minced onion	15 ml
1/2 green pepper cut in 1-inch pieces		
1/2 tsp.	salt	2-1/2 ml
dash	pepper	
1/2 tsp.	basil	2-1/2 ml
15-1/2 oz. jar	spaghetti sauce	442 g
3 slices	American processed cheese	

1. Combine beef, egg, bread, onion, green pepper, and seasonings in a large mixing bowl. Press half the mixture into a 1-1/2 qt. (8x4) loaf dish.

2. Cover this mixture with the pieces of cheese. Then cover cheese with rest of meat mixture. Pour half the spaghetti sauce over the meat loaf.

3. Place in microwave oven. Cook at FULL POWER 14-16 minutes.

4. Heat at FULL POWER remainder of spaghetti sauce in jar for 2 minutes. Let stand 10 minutes.

5. Slice 1-1/2" thick and serve with hot sauce.

Serves 4-6.

Microwave time: 16-18 minutes
Conventional range time: 45 minutes at 350°

Baked Potatoes

4 baking potatoes

1. Scrub potatoes and pierce skins with a fork.
2. Place in microwave oven leaving a 1-inch space between potatoes.
3. Cook at FULL POWER, uncovered, in microwave oven 10-12 minutes or until tender.

Serves 4.

Microwave time: 10-12 minutes
Conventional range time: 45 minutes at 450°

Crunchy Green Beans

2 16 oz. cans	green beans	454 g each
1 10-oz. can	cream of mushroom soup	300 g
1 8-oz. can	french fried onion rings	240 g
1 Tbs.	lemon juice	15 ml
2 Tbs.	chopped pimiento	30 ml

1. In a deep, 1-1/2-qt., heat-resistant, non-metallic casserole, combine cut green beans and soup. Blend well.
2. Cook, at FULL POWER, uncovered in microwave oven 5 to 7 minutes.
3. Sprinkle top of bean mixture with onion rings, lemon juice and pimiento and heat, at FULL POWER, uncovered, in microwave oven an additional 3 minutes or until garnish is heated through.

Serves 4-6.

Microwave time: 10 minutes
Conventional range time: 30 minutes at 375°

Toppings and Sauces

CHAPTER 4

There are many toppings and sauces for foods cooked in the microwave oven that substitute for the "brown look" of foods cooked in the conventional range. Piquant sauces and gourmet garnishes may be created in your microwave oven with a minimum of stirring, utensils, and time. Or, if you still prefer the "brown look" of the conventional range or broiler, you can cook food mostly in the microwave oven and transfer it to the conventional range for the last few minutes. Not only in this chapter but also scattered throughout this book are many glazes, toppings, sauces and gravies.

TOPPINGS FOR FISH, MEAT, POULTRY, VEGETABLES, AND CASSEROLES:

buttered, seasoned crumbs, browned ahead of time and stored for use

parsley, dill, chives, fresh and chopped, stored in freezer

tiny shrimp, minced clams, or baby oysters, drained and sprinkled with paprika

canned onion rings, potato chips or crackers, crushed

peppers, green or red chopped or sliced

cheese, grated, sliced or cubes

herbs, seeds, spices

tomatoes, zucchini, summer squash slices

artichokes, sliced

lemon, lime, or orange sliced

bacon, crumbled or bits

sausage or ham sliced

nuts, browned in butter, chopped

green grapes in wine sauce

mushrooms, sauteed

TOPPINGS FOR CAKES AND DESSERTS
(Many will melt and leave a glaze)

chopped nuts

coconut, toasted, plain or colored

whipped cream, plain or with a dusting of cocoa or instant coffee

peppermint sticks, crushed

chocolate-covered peppermints

candied fruit, chopped

poppy seeds

berries, whole or sliced

maple syrup, jams or jellies

granola, sweetened and crushed

lemon or orange, sliced, and fresh mint springs

cinnamon and sugar mixed

cinnamon candy red hots

jelly beans or life savers, crushed

crystallized ginger

chocolate or butterscotch bits

cookies or graham crackers, crushed

powdered sugar dusted through a lace doily

fruit jellos over a warm cake melt to a glaze.

It is probably not mere coincidence that both *trompe l'oeil* and Escoffier are French. *Trompe l'oeil* is visual deception, particularly in paintings in which objects are rendered in extremely fine detail emphasizing the illusion of tactile and spatial qualities. Auguste Escoffier (1847-1935) was a chef and author, famous for his infinite variety of sauces that transformed lowly cuts of meats by visual and gustatory deception into epicurean delights.

Sauces and gravies cook exceedingly well in the microwave oven. You need no longer fear sticking, scorching, or lumping. One or two good stirrings during the short cooking process will produce an even-textured sauce.

Sauce cooked in a low, wide casserole, cooks faster than if cooked in a deep, high casserole.

Basic Gravy

1/4 cup	rendered fat	1/16 l
3 Tbs.	flour	45 ml
1 tsp. (optional)	commercial browning and seasoning sauce	5 ml
1 tsp.	salt	5 ml
1/4 tsp.	pepper	1-1/4 ml
1 small	onion, chopped	
	water	

1. Remove meat from dish in which it has cooked. Pour drippings into a bowl and place in refrigerator, if you have the time, to allow the fat to rise to the top.
2. Skim off the fat and reserve.
3. Place 1/4 cup of fat into a 1-qt. baking dish. Heat at FULL POWER, uncovered, 3 minutes or until mixture is smooth.
4. Add flour, salt, pepper, onion, browning sauce and water to obtain the desired thickness. Heat at FULL POWER 2-3 minutes. Stir often.

Makes 2-1/2 cups.

Microwave time: 5-6 minutes
Conventional range time: 12-15 minutes

Bechamel Sauce

1 Tbs.	minced onion	15 ml
3 Tbs.	corn oil	45 ml
1/2 cup	flour	1/8 l
1 tsp.	Worcestershire sauce	5 ml
2 tsp.	soy sauce	10 ml
1 cup	cream	1/4 l
1-1/2 cups	chicken bouillon	3/8 l
1 tsp.	*fine herbs*	5 ml

1. Heat browning dish and add oil and minced onion, flour, Worcestershire sauce, soy sauce, herbs, and seasonings, stirring outside the oven after each addition until sauce thickens.

2. Scald cream in oven for 25-50 seconds. Gradually stir it into sauce until it is smooth. Add bouillon.

3. Place sauce in microwave oven and heat at FULL POWER 2 minutes, stirring twice.

4. Remove from oven and strain through a sieve. Cool and store in refrigerator. Sauce can be reheated in microwave oven in seconds!

Makes 2 cups.

Microwave time: 6-8 minutes
Conventional range time: 20-25 minutes

Mornay Sauce

2 cups	Bechamel Sauce	1/2 l
2	egg yolks	
1/2 cup	heavy cream	1/8 l
2 Tbs.	grated Parmesan cheese	30 ml
2 Tbs.	grated Gruyere cheese	30 ml
2 Tbs.	butter	30 ml

1. Heat Bechamel sauce at FULL POWER in microwave oven 2 minutes.

2. Remove from oven and gradually stir in egg yolks beaten with cream.

3. Add butter and grated cheese.

4. Return to oven for 2-4 minutes, stirring often, until sauce is smooth.

Makes 2-1/2 cups.

Green Sauce (for fish)

1 Tbs.	cooking oil	15 ml
1	medium onion, minced	
1/2 cup	chicken or vegetable bouillon	1/8 l
1/2 cup	vermouth or white wine	1/8 l
1/2 cup	parsley flakes	1/8 l
	dash of cayenne	

1. Heat oil in browning dish at FULL POWER 2 minutes. Cook onion in hot oil until brown, 2-3 minutes.
2. Add remaining ingredients, stir, cover and heat another 2 minutes at FULL POWER.
3. Strain mixture through a sieve or put in a blender for a few seconds on puree.

Makes 1 cup.

Microwave time: 4-5 minutes.
Conventional range time: 10-15 minutes.

Quick Hollandaise Sauce (for vegetables)

1/2 cup	mayonnaise	1/8 l
1-3/4 Tbs.	hot water	26-1/4 ml
1 tsp.	lemon juice	5 ml

1. Stir hot water into mayonnaise in a bowl. Place in microwave oven and heat at FULL POWER 30 seconds or until heated through.
2. Add lemon juice.

Makes 1/2 cup.

Microwave time: 30-60 seconds
Conventional range time: 10-12 minutes

Yogurt Hollandaise Sauce

2 Tbs.	butter or margarine	30 ml
1 Tbs.	all-purpose flour	30 ml
1 egg yolk		
1 cup	yogurt*	1/4 l
1 tsp.	lemon juice	5 ml
Dash cayenne		

1. Melt butter in 4-cup measure 20 seconds.

2. Add flour; mix well. Cook 1 minute at FULL POWER.

3. Add egg yolk; mix well. Gradually add yogurt, mixing well after each addition.

4. Cook at FULL POWER 2-1/2 to 3 minutes, stirring after each minute of cooking.

5. Add lemon juice and cayenne.

*See Yogurt recipe in Other Uses chapter.

Makes 1 cup.

Microwave time: 3 - 5 minutes.
Conventional range time: Approximately 10 minutes

Low-Calorie Hollandaise

1 cup	water	1/4 l
1/2 tsp.	salt	2-1/2 ml
1/2 tsp.	dry mustard	2-1/2 ml
1/2 cup	non-fat dry milk	1/8 l
2 tsp.	cornstarch	10 ml
2	egg yolks	
3 Tbs.	lemon juice	45 ml

1. Combine all ingredients except lemon juice in electric blender (or beat thoroughly) until smooth.

2. Pour into a 1-pt. measuring cup. Place in microwave oven and heat 1-1/2 minutes at FULL POWER. Stir, then heat 1-2 minutes at FULL POWER.

3. Remove and stir in lemon juice.

Makes 1-1/2 cups.

Low-Calorie: 90 calories/2 Tbs. serving.

Microwave time: 2-1/2 to 3-1/2 minutes
Conventional range time: 6-10 minutes

Spaghetti Sauce

2 lbs.	ground pork and beef or all beef	908 g
1/4 cup	olive oil	1/16 l
1 cup	mushrooms, chopped	1/4 l
1	medium onion, chopped	
1	green pepper, chopped	
1	clove garlic, minced	
1 tsp.	mustard	5 ml
1 Tbs.	sugar	15 ml
1 tsp.	oregano	5 ml
1 28-oz. can	tomatoes	795.5 g
1 15-oz. can	tomato sauce	426.1 g
2 6-oz. cans	tomato paste	170.5 g each
2 Tbs.	Worcestershire sauce	30 ml

1. Heat browning dish in oven 4 minutes. Add olive oil and brown meat in it 7-8 minutes.
2. Add mushrooms, onion, peppers, and garlic and heat 4 minutes at FULL POWER.
3. Stir in mustard, sugar, oregano, tomatoes, tomato sauce, paste, and Worcestershire sauce. Heat at FULL POWER 4 minutes.

Makes 2 quarts.
Microwave time: 15 minutes
Conventional range time: 30-40 minutes

Creole Sauce

3 Tbs.	vegetable oil	45 ml
2 Tbs.	onion, chopped	30 ml
1	small green pepper	
1/4 cup	mushrooms, sliced	1/16 l
1-3/4 cups	tomatoes	7/16 l
1/2 tsp.	salt	2-1/2 ml
	pepper	
	few drops of Tabasco	
1/2 tsp.	thyme or basil	2-1/2 ml

1. Place oil in casserole. Add onion, green pepper, and sliced mushrooms. Place in microwave oven and heat at FULL POWER 1 minute.
2. Add the rest of the ingredients and heat at FULL POWER 5 minutes more.

Makes 1-1/2 cups.
Microwave time: 6 minutes
Conventional range time: 35 minutes

Main Dishes

CHAPTER 5

MEAT

Most meats and poultry cook well in the microwave oven with less shrinkage than in conventional oven cooking. Place the meat on top of an inverted plate or microwave-safe rack so juices and fats will accumulate on the bottom of the pan for gravy. Never salt meats before cooking. Salt absorbs microwave energy and consequently toughens the surface of the meat. Cook most meat on ROAST. (70% of power) Use SIMMER (50% of power) for less tender cuts. Remember to check meats and poultry with a thermometer after cooking time has elapsed, or if your oven is equipped for it, use the automatic probe and cook to desired doneness. Allow for standing time outside the oven: cover the meats and poultry with foil and allow 5-10 minutes for smaller cuts, 10-15 minutes for larger cuts. There are many ways to achieve a brown crust. Some recipes call for browning vegetables and meats in the browning pan first. An alternative to this is to saute foods until tender in butter or oil in an ordinary oven-proof pan. Or you may add a topping or sauce (see Chapter 4 for suggestions). Or you may finish cooking under a conventional broiler, in a conventional oven, or on a barbecue.

Pork or Fresh Ham

Minutes per pound	Internal Temperature at end of Cooking Time	Internal Temperature 10-15 minutes Standing Time
8-9 mins./lb.	170° - 175° F.	180° - 185° F.

Roast Pork

4-lb.	pork loin	1.8 k
3/4 cup	stock	3/16 l
	salt and pepper	

1. Place pork roast, fat-side-down on a microwave rack or trivet in baking dish in microwave oven and cook 32-36 minutes on ROAST (70% of power). Turn over after half the heating time.

2. When roast is turned with fat-side-up, baste often with stock.

3. Salt and pepper during standing time.

Variation: Combine 3 Tbs. (45 ml) oil, 2 Tbs. (30 ml) lemon juice, 1 tsp. (5 ml) thyme, and 1 chopped clove of garlic. Baste with this mixture after roast is turned instead of basting with the stock.

Serves 6-8.

Microwave time: 32-36 minutes
Conventional range time: 2 to 2-1/4 hours at 350°

Rolled Rib Roast or Standing Rib Roast

	Minutes per pound	Internal Temperature at end of Cooking Time	Internal Temperature 10-15 minutes Standing Time
Rare:	5 min/lb.	120° - 130° F.	130° - 135° F.
Medium:	6 min/lb.	140° - 150° F.	150° - 155° F.
Well done:	7 min/lb.	160° - 165° F.	170° - 175° F.

3 lbs.		tender cut roast beef	1.4 k
		garlic cloves, peeled	
2		bay leaves	
3 Tbs.		prepared spicy mustard	45 ml
		pepper or commercial	
		browning sauce	

1. Place roast, fat-side-down on a plastic rack or trivet.
2. Rub meat with garlic and pepper and spread mustard or browning sauce over top and sides of meat.
3. Cook half of total time required. Turn roast over and finish cooking fat-side-up.

Low-calorie: 280 calories per serving.

Microwave time: 15-21 minutes
Conventional range time: 1 hour 20 minutes to 1-1/2 hours at 350°

Beef Pot Roasts (rump, chuck, shoulder, arm)

These cuts of meat vary in tenderness and should be cooked on ROAST (70% of power).

	Minutes per Pound	Internal Temperature at end of Cooking Time	Internal Temperature 10-15 Minutes of Standing Time
Medium Well	16 min/lb.	155° - 160° F.	165° - 170° F.
Well Done	18 min/lb.	160° - 165° F.	170° - 175° F.

The flavor of these cuts is improved if they are first seared in a small amount of oil on a conventional range or in a microwave browing dish.

Meat with a covering of fat should be started fat-side-down, turning over to fat-side-up after half of cooking time.

Standing times for meats are very important. Before checking to see if a roast is completely done, it should be allowed to stand at least 10-15 minutes.

Chili Con Carne

This spicy, dish is served in South America with lots of cold beer or ice water, crackers, and lettuce leaves. It freezes well too.

2 Tbs.	butter or margarine	30 ml
1	medium onion, chopped	
1	green pepper, chopped	
1 lb.	ground beef	454 g
1 lb. can	tomato sauce	454 g
1 lb. can	whole tomatoes (drained)	454 g
1 lb. can	kidney beans (drained)	454 g
1-1/2 tsp.	salt	7-1/2 ml
1/2 tsp.	red pepper (for those who like it hot)	2-1/2 ml
1/4 tsp.	black pepper	1-1/4 ml
1/4 tsp.	cumin	1-1/4 ml
2 Tbs.	chili powder	30 ml

1. Heat browning dish, 4 minutes.
2. Sauté onion and green pepper in browning dish with melted fat for 2-3 minutes. Add crumbled ground beef.
3. Place in microwave oven and heat 6 minutes at FULL POWER. Stir every two minutes.
4. Transfer to a deep, 2-qt. casserole. Add tomato sauce, tomatoes, beans, salt, pepper, cumin, and chili powder.
5. Cover and cook at FULL POWER 10-12 minutes, stirring after 5 minutes.
6. Standing time: 5 minutes.

Serves 4-6.

Microwave time: 22-25 minutes
Conventional range time: 1 hour

*If you don't own a browning dish, you may place onions and green pepper in a 2-quart casserole, crumble ground beef over it, cover and cook for 2-3 minutes at FULL POWER. Drain fat and add other ingredients. This method doesn't require additional fat thus it's lower in calories.

Norwegian Meatballs

This recipe was given to me by a Norwegian friend who claims it is better than a love potion. Every time she cooks it, her husband seems to fall in love with her all over again!

1/4 cup	dry bread crumbs	1/16 l
1/2 cup	milk, evaporated or cream	1/8 l
1/2 lb.	lean ground beef	227 g
1/2 lb.	lean ground veal	227 g
1	beaten egg	
3/4 tsp.	salt	3-3/4 ml
1/4 tsp.	white pepper	1-1/4 ml
1/2 cup	minced onion	1/8 l
2 Tbs.	capers, mashed	30 ml
3 Tbs.	flour	45 ml
1-1/3 cups	chicken stock or bouillon	1/3 l
1/3 cup	butter or pan drippings	1/12 l
1-1/2 oz.	gjetost or Swiss cheese, grated	40 g
2 Tbs.	minced parsley	30 ml

1. Pour milk or cream over bread crumbs and soak 15 minutes.
2. Blend beef and veal, egg, salt, pepper, onion, capers, and crumb mixture. Shape into 1-inch meatballs and arrange on a shallow dish.
3. Place in microwave oven and cook at FULL POWER for 8-10 minutes.
4. Rest 5 minutes and make gravy of the rest of the ingredients except the parsley which is topping. The gravy will take 3-5 minutes to cook in the microwave oven.
5. Pour gravy over meatballs and top with parsley.

Serves 4-6.

Microwave time: 11-15 minutes
Conventional range time: 30-35 minutes

Sweet and Sour Corned Beef

3 lbs.	corned beef, pickled	1.4 k
2	onion slices	
1	bay leaf	
	water	
1	clove garlic	
1/2 tsp.	marjoram	2-1/2 ml
1	stalk celery	

Sweet-Sour Sauce

2 Tbs.	butter	30 ml
5 Tbs.	catsup	75 ml
1 Tbs.	prepared mustard	15 ml
3 Tbs.	vinegar	45 ml
1/3 cup	brown sugar	1/12 l

1. Place corned beef, onions, spices, and celery in a deep, 3-qt. casserole with enough water to cover meat.
2. Cover. Place in microwave oven at SIMMER (50% of power) 50-60 minutes or until tender.
3. While meat stands, mix sweet-sour sauce in a mixing bowl and bring to a boil in microwave oven, approximately 3 minutes.
4. Drain water, spices, and vegetables from meat. Pour sweet-sour sauce over corned beef. Place in microwave oven and heat at FULL POWER for 6-8 minutes.

Serves 4-6.

Microwave time: 56-68 minutes
Conventional range time: 5 to 5-3/4 hours

Veal Chasseur

1 lb.	veal medallions	454 g
1 Tbs.	cooking oil	15 ml
2 Tbs.	lemon juice	30 ml
1 Tbs.	butter	15 ml
1/4 cup	minced onions or shallots	1/16 l
1/2 cup	mushrooms, sliced	1/8 l
2 Tbs.	tomato paste (optional)	30 ml
1/2 cup	dry white wine	1/8 l
1 cup	consommé	1/4 l
1 Tbs.	minced parsley	15 ml

1. Pound veal medallions flat.
2. Preheat browning dish 4 minutes. Add oil, and brown veal 1-2 minutes on each side. Cover.
3. Continue to cook at FULL POWER 2 minutes with lid on browning dish.
4. Remove from oven, sprinkle with lemon juice and set aside. Prepare sauce: melt butter, add onions and mushrooms. Place in microwave oven and cook at FULL POWER 1 minute. Remove from oven, stir in tomato paste, and add wine, consommé, and minced parsley. Return to oven until bubbly, about 45 seconds.
5. Pour this hot sauce over veal dish. Place veal in microwave oven and heat at FULL POWER for 1 minute just before serving.

Serves 3-4.

Microwave time: 9 to 11 minutes
Conventional range time: 30-40 minutes at 350°

Moussaka

For fewer calories, omit browning steps, and prepare in a large casserole, draining fat off meat before adding other ingredients

1	medium-sized eggplant	
2/3 cup	butter	1/16 l
1	large onion, chopped	
1-1/2 lbs.	ground lamb or beef	.7 k

2 Tbs.	tomato paste	30 ml
1/4 cup	chopped parsley	1/16 l
1/8 tsp.	cinnamon	5/8 ml
	salt and pepper to taste	
4 Tbs.	flour	60 ml
2 cups	milk	1/2 l
3	eggs, beaten well	
1 cup	ricotta cheese or cottage cheese	1/4 l
1/2 cup	bread crumbs	1/8 l
1/2 cup	Parmesan cheese	1/8 l
	nutmeg	

1. Heat browning dish 4 minutes. Peel the eggplant and cut into 1/2-inch slices. Brown in 2 Tbs. of butter in browning dish and heat for 3-4 minutes, turning once. Set aside in a bowl.

2. In the same browning dish, add 2 Tbs. of butter and brown the chopped onions for 3-4 minutes, stirring once.

3. Add the meat and cook at FULL POWER for 2-1/2 minutes. Set aside.

4. Combine tomato paste, parsley, cinnamon, salt and pepper. Stir this mixture into the meat. Place in microwave oven and heat at FULL power 5-6 minutes or until all the liquid has been absorbed. Remove dish from oven.

5. Make a white sauce by melting rest of butter in microwave oven 15-20 seconds and blending in flour until smooth.

6. Gradually stir in milk and heat at FULL POWER uncovered 2-3 minutes or until thick and smooth. Stir frequently. Remove from oven.

7. Cool mixture 5-7 minutes and stir in eggs and cheese.

8. Grease a large, 3-qt. dish and sprinkle bottom with bread crumbs. Arrange layers of eggplant and meat in its sauce with layers of Parmesan cheese and bread crumbs. Pour the cheese sauce over the top and grate nutmeg over it for a topping.

9. Place in microwave oven and cook at FULL POWER 15 minutes. Let stand before serving.

Serves 4-5.

Microwave time: 36-40 minutes.
Conventional range time: 1-1/2 hours to 2 hours at 375°

Lamb or Veal Roast

	Minutes per pound	Internal Temperature at end of Heating Time	Internal Temperature after 10-15 mins. Standing Time
Medium Well	7 - 7-1/2	155° - 160° F.	170° F.
Well Done	8 - 8-1/2	165° - 170° F.	180° F.

Roast Leg of Lamb

5 lb.	leg or shoulder of lamb (check to be sure it will fit in oven)	2.3 k
2	garlic cloves, split	
1 Tbs.	paprika	15 ml
	salt and pepper	

1. Place lamb fat-side-down on microwave rack or trivet in baking dish. Wrap last 2 inches with foil Be sure foil does not touch walls of oven. Place in microwave oven on ROAST (70% of power) 15 minutes.

2. Turn over roast, remove foil, and season by cutting wedges on top of roast and inserting garlic pieces. Rub paprika over top and sides, add salt and pepper, and baste if necessary. Return to oven to cook at FULL POWER 15-25 minutes more depending on how well done you like your lamb.

Variation: Baste with orange juice instead of lamb drippings.

Serves 6-8.

Low Calorie: 32 calories per serving.

Microwave time: 30-40 minutes
Conventional range time: 2 to 2-1/2 hours at 350°

POULTRY

Microwave cooking preserves the tenderness and moisture of poultry. The time needed to cook will vary depending on age and size of the bird. Before cooking, thaw the bird completely. Cook whole poultry uncovered, using foil to cover the thinnest parts during part of the cooking time. Don't let the foil touch the sides of the oven. For best results cook on ROAST (at 70% of power). Cover completely with foil during standing time.

Poultry Roasting Times

	Minutes per pound	Internal Temperature at end of Cooking Time	Internal Temperature at end of Standing Time
Turkey			
(8-10 lb.)	8 min./lb.	170° - 175° F.	180° - 185° F.
(10-12 lb.)	9 min./lb.		
Chicken			
(2-3 lb.)	8 min./lb.	180° - 185° F.	190° - 195° F.
(3-4 lb.)	9 min./lb.		
Cornish Game Hen			
(Whole)	8 min. /lb.	175° - 180° F.	185° - 190° F.

Insert thermometer into the thickest part of the thigh. Use a microwave thermometer in the oven during cooking. A conventional thermometer may only be used outside of the oven at the end of the cooking time.

Brush with melted butter. Place whole bird breast-side down in baking dish on an inverted saucer or microwave trivet. Turn over after half the cooking time.

Roast Turkey with Oyster Stuffing

Note the use of butter in the basting sauce. Though fat is available in the bottom of the roasting pan, butter still adds a special flavor to poultry. A Milwaukee chef, of German descent, always basted her turkeys with butter, while quoting a Bavarian adage that roughly translated as "Butter never hides itself."

1 12 lb.	turkey	5.45 k
1 tsp.	coarse salt	5 ml
1/2 tsp.	pepper	2-1/2 ml
Basting Sauce:		
1/2 cup	melted butter or margarine	1/8 l
1 Tbs.	commercial browning sauce	15 ml
1 Tbs.	white wine or sherry (optional)	15 ml
	tarragon	
Oyster Stuffing (optional):		
1 cup	butter or any good fat	1/4 l
1 cup	onions, chopped	1/4 l
3 cups	bread stuffing (unseasoned)	3/4 l
1 Tbs.	parsley, chopped	15 ml
1/2 tsp.	thyme	2-1/2 ml
1/2 tsp.	tarragon	2-1/2 ml
	salt and pepper	
3	stalks celery, chopped	
1 dozen	oysters, and some of their juice	

1. If turkey is frozen, it may be defrosted in the microwave oven according to the Defrost Chart on page 14, or it may be thawed in the refrigerator. (It is preferable to cook two 10-lb. turkeys, one after the other, in the microwave oven than one 20-lb. turkey.)

2. If you do not wish to stuff the turkey, close the openings with a slice of bread, tie legs to tail and wings together with wooden skewer or string.

3. If you wish to stuff the turkey:
a) Place butter and onions in large bowl. Cook at FULL POWER covered 2 to 3 minutes. Add bread stuffing with herbs and seasoning and continue to cook at FULL POWER 2 to 3 minutes.
b) Remove pan from oven and add celery and some juice from oysters.
c) Preheat browning dish 4 minutes.
d) While browning dish heats, drain oysters, roll in flour, then in beaten egg mixed with oil, and then in cracker crumbs. Brown in butter or oil in browning pan in microwave oven and heat at FULL POWER 1-2 minutes, turning once. The oysters must not overcook; they should be brown or golden on the outside but juicy inside.
e) Stuff the turkey with alternate layers of oysters and bread mixture. Sew cavities or close with wooden skewers.

4. Place the turkey on microwave rack or trivet in a large, shallow roasting pan, breast down. Cook at FULL POWER half of cooking time, approximately 36 minutes.

5. Combine ingredients for basting sauce.

6. Turn turkey breast-side-up and continue cooking, basting frequently with the sauce, for the remaining half of the cooking time, approximately 36 minutes more.

7. Insert microwave thermometer, or probe into meatiest portion of thigh joint, not touching fat or bone. If it does not register 170° F. return to oven for a few additional minutes until the thermometer does register 170° F.

8. Let turkey stand covered with foil at room temperature 20 to 30 minutes to finish cooking. The internal temperature should be 180° F. after standing.

Serves 12-18.

Microwave time: with stuffing, 88-90 minutes; without stuffing, 72-74 minutes
Conventional range time: 3-1/2 - 4 hours at 325°

Roast Duckling in Wine with Green Grapes

1 4-5 lb.	duckling	1.8 - 2.3 k
2 cups	stuffing (optional)	1/2 l
1 tsp.	salt (coarse kosher salt is preferable)	5 ml
1/4 tsp.	nutmeg	1-1/4 ml

Marsala Wine and Grape Sauce:

3/4 cup	marsala wine	3/16 l
2 Tbs.	grape jelly	30 ml
1-1/2 Tbs.	cornstarch	22-1/2 ml
1 cup	seedless green grapes	1/4 l

1. Wash duckling and dry. Sprinkle salt and nutmeg in the cavity. Close openings with wooden picks. Tie legs together. Tie wings to body. Wrap bits of foil over tips of legs and wings to prevent overcooking. Cover with wax paper to prevent splattering.

2. Place duckling with or without stuffing, breast-side-down in a baking dish. Cook at FULL POWER 6 minutes per pound or 24 minutes for a 4-lb. duckling. After 12 minutes, turn bird breast-side-up and drain off accumulated fat. Continue cooking.

3. Remove from microwave oven; remove foil pieces and wax paper. Drain fat.

4. Blend wine, jelly, and cornstarch together. (You may need to add a bit of water.) Heat in a measuring cup in microwave oven 45 seconds or until thick and smooth. Add the grapes and heat at FULL POWER for 45 seconds more. Pour sauce over duck.

5. Roast in conventional range for 30 minutes at 400° until skin is crispy brown and legs can be moved easily. Let stand 10 minutes.

Variation: Substitute for the wine sauce an orange sauce. Use 3/4 cup (3/16 l) orange juice and 1/2 cup (1/8 l) orange marmelade.

Serves 4-6.

Microwave time: 25-31 minutes (then 30 minutes in conventional range at 400°)
Conventional range time: 2 - 2-1/2 hours

Paella Valenciana

1 fryer chicken cut into serving pieces		
1/4 cup	butter	1/16 l
1	crushed clove of garlic	
1-1/4 cups	long-grain rice	5/16 l
1-1/2 cups	chicken stock or bouillon	3/8 l
1/2 tsp.	saffron	2-1/2 ml
1 6-oz. box	frozen lobster	165 g
1/2 lb.	medium-sized shrimp	227 g
1/2 qt.	clams in shell	.45 ml
1	hot Italian link sausage	
1 2-oz. jar	sliced pimiento	55 g
1 10-oz. package	frozen artichoke hearts	280 g
1/2 cup	sherry	1/8 l
	Parmesan cheese	

1. Heat browning dish, 4 minutes. Brown pieces of chicken in butter and garlic in browning dish. Place in microwave oven and cook at FULL POWER 7-9 minutes, covered. Turn once. Remove chicken. Set aside.

2. In juices remaining in browning dish, brown the rice, 3-4 minutes.

3. Add saffron and chicken stock and heat at FULL POWER 5-6 minutes until liquid is absorbed but rice is only partially cooked.

4. Butter the bottom and sides of a deep casserole. Put half the pieces of chicken in the casserole, cover with sliced rounds of sausage, lobster, shrimp, and clams. Add half the rice and cover again with a layer of chicken, sausage, lobster, shrimp, and clams. Add rest of rice and place in microwave oven and cook at FULL POWER 8-10 minutes, adding chicken stock from time to time, if needed. Heat at FULL POWER covered but stir occasionally.

5. Add sherry, pimiento strips, and artichokes. Top with Parmesan cheese. Cover and cook at FULL POWER 3 minutes or until artichoke hearts are done. When serving, place some of the clams in their shells on top for textural appeal and a few shrimp on top for color treatment.

Variation: Substitute crab meat for lobster, and mussels for crabs.

Serves 6.

Microwave time: 27-31 minutes
Conventional range time: 1 hour, 15 minutes - 1-1/2 hours at 350°

Stir-Fry Chicken

1 lb. (2 breasts)	chicken (or equivalent in other meat or seafood which is about 1 lb. solid meat)	454 g
1	egg white	
1 Tbs.	dry sherry	15 ml
1 Tbs.	cornstarch	15 ml
1 Tbs.	soy sauce	15 ml
2 Tbs.	peanut or vegetable oil	30 ml
2 tsp.	sesame seeds	10 ml
2-4 slices	fresh ginger root *or*	
1/4 tsp.	ground ginger	1-1/4 ml
	salt and pepper	
1/2 lb.	fresh mushrooms	227 g
1/2 clove	garlic	
1/4 cup	water chestnuts, sliced thin	1/16 l
1/4 cup	snow peas	1/16 l
2	scallions including tops *or*	
1 medium	onion	
1	green pepper	
1	red sweet pepper	
1	carrot	

1. Well ahead of time, bone, skin and cut chicken into bite-sized pieces.

2. Combine with egg white, sherry, soy sauce, cornstarch, sesame seeds and ginger. Set aside to marinate 15 minutes to 24 hours.

3. Heat browning dish, 4 minutes. Add oil. When hot, add marinated chicken.

4. Cook at FULL POWER 3-4 minutes, stirring every 30 seconds.

5. Remove from oven and place chicken in a sieve in order to drain oil from browning pan.

6. Cook vegetables beginning with the carrot, the longest cooking of the vegetables. Cook at FULL POWER 1 minute, stirring often.

7. Add remaining vegetables, stirring often. Cook at FULL POWER 30 seconds - 1 minute.

8. Add meat. Reheat entire mixture and correct seasoning.

9. If mixture appears a little dry, add more soy sauce or a

tablespoon of water. Cook at FULL POWER 3-4 minutes or until meat is done.

Serves 4.

Microwave time: 11-13 minutes
Conventional range time: 35-45 minutes

Chicken Breasts Supreme

4 chicken breasts, split, boned and skinned
Sauce

1/4 cup	butter or margarine	1/16 l
2 cups	mushroom slices	1/2 l
1 clove garlic, minced		
5 tsp.	all-purpose flour	25 ml
1/4 cup	white wine	1/16 l
1 Tbs.	lemon juice	15 ml
1/2 tsp.	tarragon	2-1/2 ml
3/4 cup	yogurt*	3/16 l

Salt and pepper

1. Place chicken pieces in dish with meatiest portions toward outside; brush with brown gravy sauce, if desired.
2. Cook at FULL POWER 14 minutes. Let stand covered with foil until ready to serve.

Sauce:

1. Melt butter in medium-sized mixing bowl 30 seconds. Add mushrooms and garlic.
2. Cook at FULL POWER 2 minutes. Remove mushrooms from butter with slotted spoon. Add flour to butter; mix well.
3. Cook at FULL POWER 1 minute. Add wine, lemon juice and tarragon.
4. Cook at FULL POWER 2 minutes, stirring after each minute of cooking. Add yogurt and mushrooms; mix well.
5. Cook at FULL POWER 2 minutes. Season to taste. Spoon sauce over warm chicken.

*See yogurt recipe in Other Uses chapter.

Serves 4.

Microwave time: 20 minutes
Conventional range time: 35-45 minutes

FISH AND SEAFOOD

Fish and seafod are more delicate, flaky, and juicy when cooked in the microwave than in a conventional range. Because there is no tough tissue in fish, cooking time is brief. Most fish and seafood should be covered during cooking and standing time. Avoid overcooking. Fish that is room temperature should be cooked one minute less than fish that has been refrigerated or frozen. After several minutes of standing time, fish should be flaked easily with a fork. Shellfish meat will appear opaque and the shell a pink color.

Baked Fish Fillets
(Salmon, Sole, Schrod, Halibut, Haddock, Flounder)

1 lb.	fish fillets	454 g
3 Tbs.	butter	45 ml
	juice of lemon (optional)	
1/2 tsp.	parsley, chopped	2-1/2 ml
1/2 tsp.	tarragon (optional)	2-1/2 ml

1. Melt butter in flat baking dish, in microwave oven and heat at FULL POWER 15 seconds.
2. Add fish. Cover. Place in microwave oven and cook at FULL POWER 4-5 minutes.
3. Turn fish once and add lemon juice and herbs for topping.
4. Let fish stand 1-2 minutes, covered.

Variation: A whole fish (11 oz.; 308 g) may be cooked in its styrofoam tray. Slit plastic cover. Place in microwave oven and heat at FULL POWER 5-6 minutes, covered. With a sauce, 8-10 minutes, covered.

Variation: For a Mock Lobster Topping that makes the most ordinary fish taste like baked, stuffed lobster, combine the following ingredients and spread over halibut, schrod, haddock, or sole fillets: 1 cup (1/4 l) Ritz crackers, crushed; 4 Tbs. (60 ml) butter, softened; salt; pepper; herbs; and juice of 1 lemon. This topping will cook along with the fish and take 1-2 minutes longer. (For an even more festive topping, add mushrooms, water chestnuts, wine, and tiny shrimp.)

Serves 3-4.

Microwave time: 4 minutes, 15 seconds – 5 minutes, 15 seconds
Conventional range time: 8-25 minutes

Sole Elegante Roll-ups

1 lb.	sole fillets	454 g
1 10-oz. can	minced clams	290 g
1/2 cup	dry white wine	1/8 l
	juice of 1/2 lemon	
1/2 cup	chopped mushrooms	1/8 l
1/4 cup	chopped onions	1/16 l
	salt and pepper	

Sauce:

1/4 cup	dry white wine	1/16 l
1/2 cup	sour cream	1/8 l
2	egg yolks, beaten	
	juice of 1/2 lemon	
1 Tbs.	butter	15 ml
1/4 cup	grated cheese	1/16 l

1. Wipe sole fillets dry and lay in a baking dish. Season with salt, pepper, and lemon juice.
2. Spread fish with minced clams (save the juice for later), chopped mushrooms, and chopped onions.
3. Roll up and secure with a toothpick.
4. Pour wine and clam juice over the roll-ups. Cover and place in microwave oven and cook at FULL POWER 4-5 minutes or until fish flakes.
5. Make the sauce in a 1-qt. (1 l) measuring cup. Blend butter, lemon juice, and sour cream together. Add the fish juice from roll-ups. Bring to a boil in the microwave oven (about 45 seconds to 1 minute).
6. Remove from oven (do not allow sauce to boil) and add beaten egg yolks.
7. Correct seasoning.
8. Pour sauce over fish, top with grated cheese, and return to oven for 1 minute or until cheese is melted.

Variations: Crabmeat, lobster, or shrimp may be used for filling. For less calories (about 155 calories per serving) substitute skim milk for sour cream and 1/2 tsp. (2-1/2 ml) mustard for butter. Omit cheese topping.

Serves 4.

Microwave time: 5-6 minutes
Conventional range time: 20-30 minutes at 350°

Shrimp Gumbo

From a 1930 book, *Good Manners,* we are instructed on the eating of soup.

Do not *tilt* your soup plate to get the last spoonful. Leave a little in the plate, if necessary. When eating soup, move the spoon AWAY from you, NEVER TOWARDS you. ALWAYS take the soup from the SIDE of the spoon! When sipping a liquid such as soup; do it QUIETLY. Do not give anyone a chance to say or think, I HEAR you like your soup.

2 cups	fresh okra, sliced	1/2 l
2 large	onions, chopped	
2 cloves	garlic, mashed	
3 Tbs.	bacon fat	45 ml
4 oz.	tomato sauce	150 g
1/4 tsp.	Tabasco sauce	1-1/4 ml
1/4 tsp.	horseradish	1-1/4 ml
1/2 lb.	hot Italian sausage, sliced	227 g
1	bay leaf	
1 tsp.	salt	5 ml
2 lbs.	raw shrimp, shelled and deveined	.9 k
3 cups	water	3/4 l

1. Combine all the above ingredients except for the shrimp. Place in casserole, cover, and cook at FULL POWER in microwave oven 5 minutes.

2. Add shrimp and cook at FULL POWER 5-7 minutes more or until shrimp are pink and tender. It should have the consistency of a thick soup. Serve over rice.

Serves 6-8.

Low calorie: 220 calories per serving

Microwave time: 10-17 minutes
Conventional range time: 45-50 minutes.

Boston Bouillabaisse

1/4 cup	olive or vegetable oil	1/16 l
1	small onion, chopped	
1 clove	garlic or	
1/8 tsp.	dehydrated garlic	5/8 ml
2 stalks	celery, chopped	
1	leek, chopped	
1	green pepper cut in strips	
2 tsps.	salt	10 ml
1/2 tsp.	fresh ground pepper	2-1/2 ml
1	bay leaf	
1/2 tsp.	thyme	2-1/2 ml
2 Tbs.	fresh chopped parsley	30 ml
2 cups	canned tomatoes	1/2 l
1 6-oz. can	tomato paste thinned with equal parts water	170 g
1 lb.	white fish in any combination cut into 1-inch chunks (scrod, haddock, turbot, or halibut)	454 g
2	meaty crablegs or	
1 6-oz. can	crabmeat	170 g
12	raw shrimp in shell or	
1 6-oz. can	shelled shrimp	170 g
1	small lobster or	
1 6-oz. can	lobster meat	170 g
12	mussels or	
12	clams in shells	
1 8-oz. can	minced clams	226.7 g
1 6-oz. bottle	clam juice	170 g
	juice from 1/2 lemon	

1. In a 4-5 qt. (3-1/2 - 4-1/2 liter) glass or ceramic bowl, combine oil, onion, garlic, leek, and celery. Place in microwave oven uncovered and cook at FULL POWER 1 minute.

2. Add remaining ingredients and mix to distribute evenly. Cook at FULL POWER 8-10 minutes more or until fish flakes. It should barely simmer.

3. Serve in a deep soup bowl.

Serves 8-10

Microwave time: 9-11 minutes
Conventional range time: 30-45 minutes

Tuna and Noodle Stroganoff

Sometimes when a new or exotic dish is served, my children or their guests will "make a face." My mother originated a response to this based on her many years of owning a restaurant. She used to say, "If you don't like it, you'll get your money back." I'm happy to say that whenever I have said these words, no one has ever asked for a refund. On the contrary, he or she usually asks for more.

1 10-oz. pouch	frozen sweet peas in butter sauce	280 g
1 5-3/4-oz. package	noodles with sour cream and cheese sauce mix	160 g
3/4 cup	milk	3/16 l
1 7-oz. can	tuna, drained and flaked	170 g
1/4 tsp.	prepared mustard	1-1/4 ml
1/2 cup	pimiento, chopped	1/8 l

1. Slit pouch of sweet peas and place in microwave oven and cook at FULL POWER 5 minutes.
2. Cook noodles at FULL POWER in water according to package directions in a bowl in microwave oven 5-6 minutes or when done. Drain well.
3. In a large 3-qt. casserole, combine peas, noodles, packet of cheese sauce mix, milk, tuna, mustard, and pimiento. Place in microwave oven and cook at FULL POWER 3-4 minutes or until heated through.

Serves 5-6.

Microwave time: 13-15 minutes
Conventional range time: 35-40 minutes at 350°

Pastas, Grains, and Breads

CHAPTER 6

PASTA AND RICE COOKING GUIDE

Cooking pasta and rice are basically rehydration processes that may not save a tremendous amount of time in the microwave oven. Nevertheless, pasta can be cooked in the microwave oven in the same container in which it is served. And rice cooked in the microwave oven never sticks or scorches. Both foods give fine results when reheated by microwaves.

For Pastas, fill a 3-quart (2-3/4 liters) container 3/4 full of water. Heat in microwave oven 6-8 minutes. Then add pasta and cook according to chart.

For Rice, use twice as much water as rice. Heat in microwave oven. Cook at FULL POWER 3-4 minutes. Then add rice and cook according to chart.

	Amount	Additions	Cook	Stand
Canelloni Lasagna Linguini Macaroni Noodles Rotini Shells, Small Spaghetti	7-8 oz. (200-227 g)	1 tsp. (5 ml) salt	7-10 min. uncovered	Drain, rinse and let stand 3-4 min., uncovered
Manicotti Shells, Jumbo	8-10 oz. (227-280 g)	1-1/2 tsp. (7-1/2 ml) salt	9-12 min. uncovered	Drain, rinse and let stand 3-4 min., covered

Spaghetti,
  Elbow or Rings
    Vermicelli
	10-12 oz.
	(280-340 g)
				Standing time is
				unnecessary when
				pasta is to be
				used in casserole

Rice, Long Grain	1 cup (1/4 l)	1 tsp. (5 ml) oil or butter	12-13 min. coverd	5 min. Stir gently with fork
Rice, Quick- Cooking	1-1/2 cups (1/3 liter)	1 tsp. (5 ml) salt	5 min., covered	

Rice, Wild
  and White
  Mix
	6-oz.
	(170 g)
	package
		2 tsp.
		(10 ml)
		butter
			15 min.
			covered
				5 min., covered

Couscous

This is a North African and Israeli dish used as an accompaniment to a meat or fish entree or as a main dish mixed with peas, mushrooms, or tomato sauce and cheese.

2 Tbs.	butter or oil	30 ml
1 small	onion, chopped	
1 cup	couscous, already toasted	1/4 l
2 cups	water or broth from	1/2 l
	bouillon cubes, meat,	
	chicken or vegetable	
pinch	salt and pepper	
	cumin or basil	

1. Heat browning dish in microwave oven 3 minutes. Melt butter or oil in it and brown onions and cook at FULL POWER 1-3 minutes, turning once.

2. Add couscous, seasoning, spices, and water. Cover. Place in microwave oven and cook at FULL POWER 2-4 minutes, stirring occasionally and adding water if necessary.

Serves 4-6.

Microwave time: 6-10 minutes
Conventional range time: 16-20 minutes

Cooked Ground Soybeans

3/4 cup	dry soybeans	3/16 l
3/4 tsp.	salt	3-3/4 ml
	water as needed	

1. Soak beans overnight in enough salted water to cover.

2. In the morning, drain and grind beans in food chopper, using medium knife. The ground beans resemble creamed corn.

3. Place in a large, 2-qt. covered casserole with 1/2 cup (1/8 liter) of water in microwave oven and cook at FULL POWER for 5 minutes or until beans become soft. Stir occasionally.

Makes 2 - 2-1/2 cups

Microwave time: 5 minutes
Conventional range time: 1 hour

Zen Buddhists regard both the preparation and eating of grains as sacred. The monks who are allowed to work in the kitchen of the monastery base all food combinations on yin (acidity) and yang (alkalinity). They also believe that a bright color near a grain is like spiritual music. Thus, a green sprig of parsley makes a bowl of brown rice happier and a red radish vivifies the whiteness of millet.

Fruit-Noodle Kugel

1 8-oz. package	broad noodles	227 g
2 qts.	water	2 l
1 tsp.	salt	5 ml
3	eggs, beaten	
1/4 cup	sugar	1/16 l
1 tsp.	cinnamon	5 ml
1/4 cup	melted salted butter	1/16 l
1 tsp.	vanilla	5 ml
1 cup	sour cream	1/4 l
1/4 cup	milk	1/16 l
1 lb.	creamed cottage cheese	454 g
1 8-oz. can	fruit cocktail, drained	227 g

cornflake topping:

1/2 cup	cornflakes	1/8 l
3 tsp.	butter	15 ml
1/2 tsp.	cinnamon	2-1/2 ml

1. Place noodles in hot water, (previously heated in oven for 3 minutes, in large, 3-qt. casserole) in microwave oven and cook at FULL POWER 4 minutes. Drain water from noodles.

2. Mix eggs, sugar, cinnamon, butter, vanilla, sour cream, milk, cottage cheese, and fruit cocktail together and then blend with cooked noodles. Set in microwave oven and cook at FULL POWER 12 minutes.

3. Mix cornflakes and cinnamon. Top casserole with this mixture and dot with butter. Continue to cook at FULL POWER 3-5 minutes more.

Serves 6-8.

Microwave time: 25-28 minutes
Conventional range time: 1 hour at 325°

Recently seen walking down Oxford Street in London was a man bearing a sandwich-board sign with the legend, "Less lust, with less meat, bird, fish, cheese, and sitting." Evidently he is an evangical vegetarian who believes in the benefices of grains.

Granola Muffins

1 cup	flour	1/4 l
1 tsp.	soda	5 ml
1 tsp.	salt	5 ml
1 cup	bran	1/4 l
1 cup	granola	1/4 l
1/2 cup	milk	1/8 l
1/2 cup	molasses	1/8 l
1	egg	
1/4 cup	raisins	1/16 l
1/4 cup	chopped nuts	1/16 l
1/2 cup	apricot jam or orange marmalade	1/8 l
	cinnamon and sugar (optional)	

1. Mix flour, soda, and salt together.

2. Add bran, granola, molasses, milk and egg.

3. Stir until just mixed. Do not beat or over-stir.

4. Add nuts and raisins.

5. Fill custard cups or microwave muffin pans only 1/2 full and make a dent in each one.

6. Fill with 1 Tbs. apricot jam or orange marmalade. Shake cinnamon and sugar over top, if desired. Let stand 10-15 minutes.

7. Cook in microwave oven 4-6 minutes at FULL POWER.

Makes 12 muffins

Microwave time: 4-6 minutes
Conventional range time: 30-40 minutes at 375°

Wheat and Noodle Pilaf (Bulghour and Noodles)

This is easy and different to serve with most entrees.

2 Tbs.	butter	30 ml
2 handfuls	thin, small noodles	
1 cup	cracked wheat, coarse grained	1/4 l
1-1/2 cups	broth, chicken or meat bouillon cubes	3/8 l

1. Heat browning dish in microwave oven 4 minutes. Melt butter in it and brown the noodles in it and heat 1-3 minutes, stirring often.

2. Add wheat and broth and cover. Cook at FULL POWER 5 minutes.

Serves 4-6.

Microwave time: 10-12 minutes
Conventional range time: 25-30 minutes

Sea Island Rice

This rice dish brought by the Gullahs, Blacks who became slaves on the Sea Islands in Georgia, is closely related to its African ancestor in its use of nuts, herbs, and oil.

1/4 cup	red pistachio nuts, shelled	1/16 l
1 cup	uncooked rice	1/4 l
2 cups	water	1/2 l
2 Tbs.	butter	30 ml
1/2 tsp.	salt	2-1/2 ml
1/4 cup	celery	1/16 l
1/4 cup	chopped parsley	1/16 l

1. Combine all the above ingredients in a deep, 2-qt. casserole and cover. Place in microwave oven and cook at FULL POWER 12-13 minutes, stirring occasionally.

2. Add more water or butter during a standing time if rice becomes dry.

Serves 4.

Microwave time: 12-13 minutes
Conventional range time: 20-30 minutes

Anadama Bread

A few years ago there was a Massachusetts bakery called Anadama that baked Anadama bread exclusively. My younger son used to loll over breakfast reading, rereading, and relishing the story, on the wrapper, of how the bread got its name. It told of a Rockport fisherman whose lazy wife, Anna, always gave him steamed corn meal mush and molasses for dinner. One day, in a rage over this monotonous fare, he mixed the mush and molasses with bread flour and yeast. As he baked it in the oven, he kept mumbling, "Anna, damn her." The bread was so tasteful that his neighbors asked for the recipe and named it Anadama Bread.

2 cups	hot water	1/2 liter
1/2 cup	cornmeal	1/8 l
1 tsp.	salt	5 ml
3/4 cup	molasses	3/16 l
8 Tbs.	butter or margarine	1/8 l
1 package	dry yeast	
1/2 cup	warm water (105°-115°)	1/8 l
4-1/2 to 5 cups	all-purpose flour	1-1/8 to 1-3/4 l

1. In a 3-quart bowl, combine water, cornmeal and salt. Cook at FULL POWER in microwave oven 3 minutes, stir; cook 3 more minutes at FULL POWER. Stir, cover and let stand 5 minutes.

2. Stir in molasses and shortening; let cool to lukewarm.

3. In a 3-quart bowl, dissolve yeast in warm water. Stir in cooled cornmeal mixture; mix well. Gradually add flour to make a stiff dough.

4. Turn onto lightly floured board; knead until smooth (7 or 8 minutes).

5. Place in greased bowl, turning to grease all surfaces. cover and let rise in a warm place (85°) until doubled in bulk (about 1 hour).

6. Punch down; shape into two round loaves; place in two well-greased 8-inch round glass cake pans or casseroles.

7. Cover and let rise again about 1 hour.

8. Bake each loaf on SIMMER (50% of power), in microwave oven 10 to 12 minutes.

9. Let stand in pan 5 minutes; turn out and cool on racks.

Makes 2 loaves.

Microwave time: 10-12 minutes
Conventional range time: 45 minutes at 375°

Vegetables

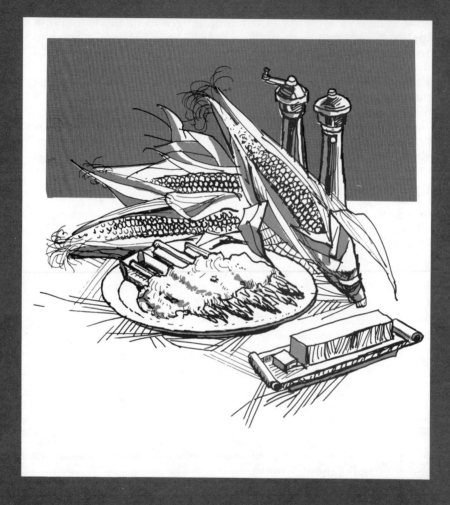

CHAPTER 7

Microwave cooking retains more of the color, flavor and nutritional value of vegetables. They become so irresistable that even the most finicky eaters find them hard to refuse. Since very small amounts of water are used to cook vegetables in your microwave oven, it is rarely necessary to drain before serving.

In this chapter you will find recipes for vegetables, plain and fancy. Note in the cooking charts for some fresh vegetables, that microwave cooking time does not differ much from conventional range cooking time. But remember that in the end you will still be minutes ahead by cooking vegetables in your microwave oven because you need not cook and drain the vegetables in a pot and then transfer them to a serving bowl. You need only to cook them in the serving bowl. The water used in cooking will have quickly evaporated and your vegetables will be tender but crisp (*al dente*) and ready to eat.

FROZEN VEGETABLE COOKING CHART

Most frozen vegetables need little or no water added. Ice crystals often provide enough moisture for cooking; rarely is more than 1/4 cup of the water needed. Frozen vegetables may be cooked directly in the paper carton if slit before cooking.

Place vegetables in a serving dish. Add water and cover with plastic wrap. Add 2 Tbs. (30 ml) hot water to Brussel Sprouts, Cauliflower, Peas, Peas & Carrots, Spinach and Squash. Add 1/4 cup (1/16 l) hot water to Corn cut off the cob.

Cook the following vegetables 3-6 mins. (covered).

Artichoke Hearts	Corn, cut off the cob
Asparagus, green spears	Corn, cream style
Beans, green diagonal-cut	Peas, green
Beans, green French	Peas & Carrots
Brussel Sprouts	Spinach, leaf or chopped
Cauliflower	Squash, Hubbard

Pouches must be slit.

Cook the following vegetables 6-10 mins. (covered). For corn on the cob cook approximately 4 mins/ear.

Beans, green cut or wax French cut	Corn, on the cob
	Okra
Beans, lima, ford hook	Onions, in cream
Broccoli, cut or spears	Peas, black-eyed
Carrots, cut or nuggets shoe peg	Vegetables, mixed

FRESH VEGETABLE COOKING CHART

Prepare vegetables. Add water and salt, cover and cook on FULL POWER. Pierce baked white and sweet potatoes and acorn squash.

Cook the following vegetables 4-8 mins.

Artichokes	2 medium
Asparagus	15 stalks (3/4 lb.)
Beans	1 lb.
Beans, lima	1 lb. (2 cups shelled)
Brussel Sprouts	1/2 lb. (2 cups)
Cabbage	1 medium head
Carrots	4 medium sliced
Cauliflower	1 medium head
Celery	4 cups sliced (6 stalks)
Corn, on cob	2-4 ears
Eggplant	1 medium
Onions	2 large
Parsnips	4 medium
Peas, green	2 cups
Spinach	10 oz.
Squash, Acorn	1 lb.
Tomatoes	4 large
Zucchini or Summer Squash	2 medium

Cook the following vegetables 7-11 mins.

Broccoli	1 small bunch (1-1/2 lb.)
Rutabaga	1 lb.
Turnips	2 or 3 medium

Cook the following vegetables 11-17 mins.

Beans, yellow wax	1 lb.
Beets (whole)	4 medium
Potatoes, baked or boiled	4 medium
Potatoes, Sweet	2 medium

Cover vegetables while cooking to help steam them in the smallest possible amount of water. Since salt tends to dehydrate and toughen microwave-cooked vegetables, add salt after cooking.

Commercially canned vegetables heat rapidly. Draining part of the liquid before cooking will shorten heating times.

Vegetables should be removed from the oven when still slightly firm. They will continue to cook during the necessary standing time, still covered, for a few minutes before serving.

Apple Red Cabbage

1 2-1/2 lb. head	red cabbage	1 liter
2 medium	onions	
1/2 cup	margarine or butter	1/8 l
1/4 cup	sugar	1/16 l
2 to 3 medium	apples, chopped	
1/3 cup	red wine vinegar	1/12 l
1-1/2 tsp.	salt	7-1/2 ml
1/4 tsp.	pepper	1-1/2 ml
1/2 tsp.	ground ginger	2-1/2 ml
3	cloves	
1/2 cup	raisins	1/8 l

1. Cut the cabbage in half lengthwise and shred into thin strands. Discard core. Peel and chop onion fine.
2. Melt margarine or butter in a 3-qt. casserole or browning dish.
3. Add onion and heat, stirring often until yellowed, 2 minutes.
4. Add sugar and stir until it begins to caramelize, 2-3 minutes.
5. Add cabbage, apple, vinegar, salt, pepper, ginger, and cloves.
6. Cover and cook at FULL POWER 5 minutes.
7. Add raisins and cook at FULL POWER until cabbage is crisp-tender, apples are cooked through and juices are reduced, 1-2 minutes.

Serves 6.

Microwave time: 10-12 minutes
Conventional range time: 35 minutes

Acorn Squash with Honey and Spiced Apples

4	small acorn squash	
	salt	
8 Tbs.	butter or margarine	120 ml
8 Tbs.	honey	120 ml
8 Tbs.	brown sugar	120 ml
1 14-oz. jar	spiced apple rings	400 g

1. Wash and dry squash.
2. Place squash in microwave oven and heat, at FULL POWER, uncovered, 15 minutes or until they feel soft to the touch.
3. Let stand 5 minutes.
4. Cut in half and remove seeds.
5. Place cut-side-up in a shallow, heat-resistant, non-metallic dish.
6. Sprinkle with salt. Place 1 Tbs. (15 ml) butter, 1 Tbs. (15 ml) brown sugar, and 1 Tbs. (15 ml) of honey in each half.
7. Cook at FULL POWER uncovered in microwave oven 4 minutes or until butter has melted.
8. Decorate platter or dish with spiced apple rings.

Serves 6-8.

Microwave time: 18-20 minutes
Conventional range time: 45 minutes at 350°

Bavarian Baked Potatoes

4	baking potatoes	
1 cup	creamy cottage cheese	1/4 l
3/4 cup	plain yogurt*	3/16 l
1/4 cup	finely chopped onion	1/16 l
1-1/2 tsp.	salt	7-1/2 ml
dash	pepper	
1/4 cup	slivered almonds	1/16 l
1/4 cup	butter or margarine	1/16 l

1. Scrub potatoes and pierce skins with fork. Bake at FULL POWER 13-15 minutes, or until tender. Wrap in foil; let stand 2-3 minutes.

2. Cut each potato in half, lengthwise; with a spoon remove the potato pulp, leaving a thin shell intact.

3. Mash potato; add cottage cheese, yogurt, onion, salt and pepper; blend until smooth. Divide potato mixture evenly among shells. Place potatoes on serving dish.

4. Heat almonds and butter 1-1/2 minutes or until golden brown. Sprinkle each potato with toasted almonds. Potatoes may be refrigerated at this point; after refrigeration, increase cooking time 2 minutes.

5. Cook at FULL POWER 6 minutes.

Serves 4.

*See Yogurt recipe in Other Uses chapter

Microwave time: 20 minutes
Conventional range time: 95 minutes

To...[Columbus] the modern table owes more than to any other that can be named. The discovery of America has enriched our tables with the turkey, cocoa, vanilla, the Jerusalem artichoke, the sugar-cane, red pepper, and a host of good things. Yet the master-cooks of Europe, who lavish their honours on nobodies and confuse their cookery books with a mob of ridiculous names, have not thought it worth their while to consecrate a single dish to his memory — not even the humble egg which he taught his friends to set on end.
— from Kettner's *Book of the Table*, 1877

Corn on the Cob Columbus

The flavor of microwave-cooked corn on the cob is redolent of the old American Indian recipe for roasting corn in the husk in a pit covered with layers of earth and burning wood. The microwave oven is the only modern cooking device that has reproduced that authentic, unique recipe successfully.

4 ears fresh corn, unhusked
Butter or margarine

1. Peel back the husks and remove the silk, leaving the husks intact.
2. Brush the ears with melted butter. Replace the husks and fasten with string or rubber bands.
3. Place in microwave oven, leaving at least 1-inch between ears. Cook at FULL POWER 4 minutes.
4. Turn ears over and cook an additional 4 minutes. Allow to stand 2 to 3 minutes with the husks in place.
5. Turn back the husks and use as a handle. Season corn to taste.

Variation: If desired, husks can be removed and corn wrapped in wax paper or placed in covered casserole and cooked as in recipe above.

Serves 4.

Microwave time: 10-11 minutes
Conventional range time: 20-22 minutes

Stuffed Peppers

Peppers are versatile vegetables. Low in calories (15 calories a pod), high in vitamins, they can be filled with leftover meat, fish, vegetables, ground beef, dried cheese, and cooked rice, combined with other ingredients.

4 medium-sized	green peppers	
2 cups	whole kernel corn	1/2 l
1/2 cup	chopped onion	1/8 l
1 cup	condensed tomato soup	1/4 l
	or tomato paste	
4 slices	cheese, American or	
	Cheddar, for topping	
	season to taste	

1. Remove tops and seeds from peppers. Place shells in a large 2-qt. bowl and cover. Heat at FULL POWER 2-4 minutes depending on the size of the peppers. They should be partially cooked.
2. Combine corn, onion, 1/2 cup of tomato soup, and seasonings.
3. Fill peppers with this stuffing. Top each with a slice of cheese.
4. Place casserole in oven and cook at FULL POWER 3-4 minutes.
5. Add remaining soup and cook at FULL POWER for another 4 minutes.

Variation: Stuff peppers with the following: 1 cup (1/4 l) cooked rice and wild rice with herb seasoning, 1 cup (1/4 l) diced, left-over chicken, 1/2 cup (1/8 l) cream, and salt and pepper.

Serves 4.

Microwave time: 9-12 minutes
Conventional range time: 50 minutes at 350°

Sauteed Mushrooms

1 lb.	fresh mushrooms	454 g
4 Tbs.	butter or margarine	60 ml
2 Tbs.	flour	30 ml
1/4 cup	sherry	1/16 l

1. Heat browning dish 4 minutes. Melt butter or margarine in browning dish 1 minute.
2. Add mushrooms, either whole or sliced, depending on their size. Season with salt.
3. Cook at FULL POWER for 2 minutes. Pour off some juice.
4. Sprinkle flour through mushrooms.
5. Stir until flour is thoroughly blended. Add sherry to this.
6. Cook at FULL POWER 2 minutes more, or until thickened.

Serves 4.

Microwave time: 8-10 minutes
Conventional range time: 15 minutes

Scalloped Tomatoes

2 cups	onion, thinly sliced	1/2 l
3/4 cup	bread cubes	1/6 l
2 Tbs.	shortening	30 ml
2 tsp.	salt	10 ml
1/2 tsp.	celery salt	2-1/2 ml
1/4 tsp.	pepper	1-1/4 ml
2 Tbs.	brown sugar	30 ml
2 cups	canned tomatoes	1/2 l

1. Heat browning dish 4 minutes. Heat shortening 30 seconds at FULL POWER.
2. Brown onions 2 minutes. Add bread cubes and brown 2 minutes more.
3. Remove bread cubes. Set aside.
4. Mix all ingredients together in casserole.
5. Top with bread cubes which were browned.
6. Cook at FULL POWER 8-10 minutes.

Serves 6.

Microwave time: 16-1/2 to 18-1/2 minutes
Conventional range time: 1 hour

Ratatouille

1-1/2 lbs.	eggplant, cut into 1/2 inch cubes	681 g
2 small (1 lb.)	zucchini, thinly sliced	454 g
1/4 cup	olive oil	1/16 l
2 medium	onions, thinly sliced	
1 clove	garlic, peeled and crushed	
1 large	green pepper, thinly sliced	
3 large	ripe tomatoes, washed and cut into 8 wedges each	
2 tsp.	dried basil leaves	10 ml
2 tsp.	dried marjoram leaves	10 ml
1 tsp.	salt	5 ml
1/2 tsp.	pepper	2-1/2 ml
1 8-oz. can	sliced mushrooms, drained	240 g

1. In a large bowl, cover eggplant and zucchini with salted water (about 1 tsp. to 1 qt. water). Soak for 30 minutes; drain.

2. In a deep, 3-qt., heat-resistant, non-metallic casserole, cook at FULL POWER olive oil, onions, and garlic, uncovered, in microwave oven 5 minutes or until onions and garlic are tender.

3. Add green pepper, drained eggplant and zucchini.

4. Cook at FULL POWER, covered, in microwave oven 5 minutes.

5. Add remaining ingredients and stir to combine well.

6. Cook at FULL POWER, uncovered, in microwave oven 5 minutes longer or until vegetables are tender.

7. Ratatouille may be served either hot or cold.

Serves 6-8.

Microwave time: 15 minutes
Conventional range time: 30 minutes

Zucchini Au Gratin

Most adults, in recalling their childhood dislikes of food, recall hiding some vegetable in the laundry hamper, tossing it down the laundry chute, or squeezing it into a pocket. Perhaps they would not have done this had the vegetables been dressed with an interesting soup sauce (cream of mushroom, celery, cheese) or one of the many sauces suggested in Chapter 4.

Here is a delicious way to prepare highly flavored and sometimes unpopular vegetables.

2 medium-sized (8-oz. each)	zucchini	224 g
3 Tbs.	water	45 ml
2 Tbs.	butter	30 ml
2 Tbs.	flour	30 ml
1/2 tsp.	salt	2-1/2 ml
1 cup	milk	1/4 l
1 cup	grated sharp Cheddar cheese	1/4 l
	paprika	

1. Wash zucchini and slice into 1/4″ pieces.
2. Place zucchini slices and water into a deep, 2-qt. casserole.
3. Cook at FULL POWER, covered, in microwave oven 4 to 6 minutes. Set aside.
4. In a medium-sized bowl, melt butter, uncovered, in microwave oven 15 seconds.
5. Blend in flour and salt. Stir until smooth. Gradually add milk.
6. Cook at FULL POWER uncovered in microwave oven for 1 minute. Stir. Cook at FULL POWER an additional 1-1/2 minutes or until sauce is thickened and smooth. Stir occasionally. Stir grated cheese into sauce.
7. Pour sauce over zucchini and cook at FULL POWER, uncovered, in microwave oven 1 minute or until zucchini is heated through.
8. Sprinkle paprika over sauce before serving.

Variation: Squash, broccoli, or cauliflower may be substituted.

Serves 4.

Microwave time: 7-9 minutes
Conventional range time: 21-25 minutes

Desserts

CHAPTER 8

For success with your microwaved cakes here are some tips:
Grease non-metallic, heat-resistant pans. Fill pans half-full. Use the left-over batter for cupcakes or a small cake. Remember to undercook cakes and bars. They are done when moist on top but dry to the probe of a toothpick in the center. Use glazes and toppings, suggested throughout this book, to cover the light-colored, moist surface. If the cake dries out a bit, a minute of reheating in the microwave oven will restore moisture and fluffiness.

While pie crusts are very flaky when cooked in the microwave oven, you may want to brown them first in a conventional oven or color the crust while mixing it by adding a few drops of yellow coloring. Remember that pies with custard or pudding fillings continue to cook during standing time. Remove them before the filling has set. Should it not become firm during standing time, you can always return it to the oven for a few seconds more of cooking.

Pistachio Cake

A green cake with a pale green frosting! This cake is a surprise and a little unusual.

1 17 to 18-1/2 oz. pkg.	white cake mix	500 g
1 2-1/2 oz. pkg.	pistachio instant pudding	99 g
4	eggs	
1/2 cup	salad oil	1/8 l
3/4 cup	club soda	3/16 l
Frosting:		
1 3-1/2 oz. pkg.	pistachio instant pudding	99 g
1 1-1/2 oz. packet	artificial whipped topping mix	45 g
1-1/2 cups	milk	1/3 l

1. Beat all ingredients for cake together. Fold into a lightly greased and floured tube pan. Let stand for 10-15 minutes.

2. Microwave on FULL POWER 10-13 minutes or until top is still wet-looking but toothpick comes out dry.

3. While cake is standing, mix frosting ingredients together. Frost cake as soon as it has cooled.

Makes 1 cake.

Microwave time: 10-13 minutes
Conventional range time: 45-50 minutes at 350°

Yellow Fruit Cake

A friend from northern Vermont perpetuates an old Yankee tradition of stirring Christmas fruit-cake batter after Thanksgiving dinner. When she was little, in the days before electric mixers, her mother would assemble quantities of ingredients for fruit cake near a 15-gallon pail. Immediately after Thanksgiving dinner, everyone, including the smallest child, took his/her turn mixing and stirring the heavy batter while making a wish. Afterwards, the family gathered around the dining room table to talk about what each hoped to receive at Christmas. Of course, everyone got his/her wish, plus a home-make fruit cake! Now my friend's daughter, who lives in Pennsylvania, is continuing the fruit-cake stirring tradition in her home.

1/2 lb.	butter or margarine	227 g
1 cup	sugar	1/4 l
3	eggs	
2-1/4 tsp.	baking powder	11-1/4 ml
1 cup	yellow cornmeal	1/4 l
1/2 tsp.	salt	2-1/2 ml
1/2 cup	candied citron and pineapple, chopped	1/8 l
1/2 cup	sultanas or yellow raisins	1/8 ml
2 Tbs.	brandy extract	30 ml

1. Cream together butter and sugar until light and fluffy.
2. Add 3 whole eggs, one at a time, beating well after each addition.
3. Sift together dry ingredients.
4. Add dry ingredients to butter and sugar mixture. Blend well.
5. Fold in candied fruits, which have been lightly floured so that they do not all settle at the bottom of the pan.
6. Add brandy extract. Grease and lightly flour an 8-9" tube pan or two small loaf pans. Add mix and let stand 10-15 minutes.
7. Microwave at FULL POWER 7 minutes. Test with toothpick to see if cake is done. If toothpick comes out with batter, cook at FULL POWER one minute more. If not, cake is done. Let stand 10 minutes and invert on rack.

Serves 10-12.

Microwave time: 7-8 minutes
Conventional range time: 50-60 minutes at 300°

Blueberry Coffee Cake

1/4 cup	butter	1/16 l
3/4 cup	sugar	3/16 l
1	egg	
1-1/2 cups	flour	3/8 l
1 tsp.	baking powder	5 ml
1/2 tsp.	nutmeg	2-1/2 ml
1/2 cup	milk	1/8 l
1 cup	blueberries, fresh or frozen	1/4 l

1. Cream butter, sugar, and egg together.
2. Sift dry ingredients together.
3. Add milk and dry ingredients alternately to the butter mixture.
4. Fold blueberries into this stiff batter.
5. Pour batter into a greased and lightly floured 8" square dish. Let stand 10-15 minutes.
6. Microwave at FULL POWER 4 minutes.

Makes 1 cake.

Microwave time: 4 minutes
Conventional range time: 25-30 minutes at 350°

Marshallow Glaze

1/3 cup	sugar	1/2 l
3 Tbs.	water	45 ml
1cup	marshamallow creme	1/3 l

1. Combine sugar and water in small mixing bowl; Heat on FULL POWER until boiling. (About 1/2 minute.)
2. Blend in marshamallow creme; add hot water 1 teaspoon at a time if thinner glaze is desired.

Makes 1 cup

Microwave time: 1 minute
Conventional range time: 5 minutes

Astronauts' Orange Pudding Cake

One of the necessities of life that the astronauts took with them to the moon was instant breakfast drink, in a natural orange flavor. Here is a pudding cake, full of vitamin C and the kind of pep that propelled the astronauts to the moon and back.

3/4 cup	sugar	3/16 l
1/4 cup	butter	1/16 l
1 tsp.	vanilla	5 ml
1-1/4 cups	flour	5/16 l
1 tsp.	baking powder	5 ml
1/4 tsp.	salt	1-1/4 ml
1/2 cup	milk	1/8 l

Topping:

1/2 cup	sugar	1/8 l
1/2 cup	instant breakfast drink, orange flavor	1/8 l
1 Tbs.	grated orange peel	15 ml
1 cup	water	1/4 l

1. Cream sugar, butter, and vanilla together.
2. Sift flour, baking powder, and salt together and add to creamed mixture, alternating with milk.
3. Spread in 8" square dish that has been lightly greased and floured.
4. Shake sugar evenly over dough.
5. Sprinkle on the instant breakfast drink.
6. Pour the water and orange peel evenly over the top.
7. Microwave at FULL POWER 4-6 minutes or until cake seems done. There will be thick orange sauce on the bottom.
8. Serve warm and top with ice cream if desired.

Makes 1 cake.

Microwave time: 4-6 minutes
Conventional range time: 30 minutes at 350°

Hot Buttered Rum Cake

This is the queen of cakes. It is elegant to look at and memorable in flavor!

1 cup	chopped pecans	1/4 l
1 18-1/2-oz. pkg.	yellow cake mix	500 g
1 3-1/2 oz.	instant vanilla pudding	99 g
1/2 cup	white rum	1/8 l
1/4 cup	water	1/16 l
1/2 cup	vegetable oil	1/8 l
4	eggs	

Rum Glaze:

1 cup	sugar	1/4 l
1/4 cup	white rum	1/16 l
1/4 lb.	butter	113 g
1/4 cup	water	1/16 l

1. Grease and flour thoroughly a microwave-safe tube or bundt pan.
2. Cover bottom and sides with chopped pecans, reserving a generous amount for the top of the cake.
3. Put all ingredients in a large bowl and beat on high speed for 2 full minutes.
4. Pour into pan. Fill pan only 2/3 full. Use remainder of batter for cupcakes. Sprinkle remaining nuts on top. Allow batter to stand 10-15 minutes.
5. Microwave at FULL POWER 6 minutes or until sides of cake begin to draw away from pan.
6. Remove cake to cool while preparing the glaze.
7. Mix all ingredients of rum glaze in deep glass bowl. Microwave at FULL POWER 3 minutes.
8. Pour over hot cake slowly. Allow cake to cool in pan before serving.

Makes 1 cake and a few cupcakes.

Microwave time: 6 minutes
Conventional range time: 1 hour at 350°

Raspberry Cheesecake

18	Zwieback crackers, crushed	
3 Tbs.	butter or margarine	45 ml
1 Tbs.	sugar	15 ml
2 8-oz. packages	cream cheese	227 g each
1/2 cup	sugar	1/8 l
2	egg yolks	
1 tsp.	grated orange peel	5 ml
1 Tbs.	lemon juice	15 ml
2	egg whites, stiffly beaten	
1 cup	commercial sour cream	1/4 l
2 Tbs.	sugar	30 ml
1 tsp.	vanilla extract	5 ml
1 16-oz. package	frozen raspberries or	454 g
1 pint	fresh raspberries, washed and hulled	

1. Lightly grease a 9-inch, heat-resistant, non-metallic baking dish.
2. In a small bowl, combine cracker crumbs, softened butter or margarine, and the 1 Tbs. (15 ml) sugar. Press into the bottom of a greased baking dish.
3. Heat at FULL POWER, uncovered, in microwave oven 2 minutes. Set aside.
4. In a large mixing bowl, beat cream cheese and the 1/2 cup (1/8 l) sugar together until light and fluffy. Add egg yolks, 1 at a time, beating well after each addition. Beat in orange peel and juice.
5. Fold in stiffly beaten egg whites. Pour into prepared baking dish; smooth with a spatula.
6. Microwave at FULL POWER 6 minutes.
7. In a small bowl, combine sour cream, the 2 Tbs. (30 ml) sugar and vanilla until well-blended. Carefully spread over top of cheesecake.
8. Microwave uncovered at FULL POWER 1 minute.
9. Arrange raspberries on cheesecake as desired and chill several hours before serving.

Serves 8.

Microwave time: 9 minutes
Conventional range time: 30-40 minutes at 325°

Colorado Chocolate Cake

This is a rich chocolate pudding cake baked together with its unusual topping.

3/4 cup	sugar	3/16 l
1-1/4 cups	flour	5/16 l
1 tsp.	baking powder	5 ml
1/8 tsp.	salt	5/8 ml
1 oz.	square unsweetened chocolate	28 g
2 tsp.	butter	30 ml
1/4 cup	milk	1/16 l
1 tsp.	vanilla	5 ml

Topping:

1/2 cup	brown sugar	1/8 l
1/2 cup	white sugar	1/8 l
4 Tbs.	cocoa	60 ml
1 cup	cold coffee	1/4 l

1. Sift dry ingredients together in a bowl.
2. Melt chocolate and butter in 9″ x 9″ dish and heat in microwave oven at FULL POWER 1 minute.
3. Add dry ingredients alternately with milk to the chocolate-butter mixture, mixing all by hand.
4. Add vanilla.
5. Spread in 9″ square pan.
6. Scatter topping ingredients on top of batter in order given.
7. Microwave at FULL POWER 4-5 minutes. Let stand 10 minutes.

Makes 1 cake.

Microwave time: 4-5 minutes
Conventional range time: 30 minutes at 350°

Apple Walnut Pudding Cake (Cholesterol-Free)

"Is it better to be the lover or the loved one? Neither, if your cholesterol is over 600." — Woody Allen

Here is an apple walnut pudding cake that a friend has devised for her husband, who is on a low-cholesterol diet. She substitutes egg substitute and corn oil for eggs and butter or saturated foods. Originally 2 teaspoons (10 ml) of baking powder were required. But baking powder is so enthusiastic in the microwave oven that it was reduced to 1 teaspoon (5 ml). (These rules for low-cholesterol bakery can be followed in converting other cakes to the microwave oven.)

4 cups	chopped, peeled apples	1 l
1-3/4 cups	sugar	7/16 l
1/2 cup	egg substitute	1/8 l
1/2 cup	corn oil	1/8 l
2 tsp.	vanilla	10 ml
2 cups	sifted flour	1/2 l
1 tsp.	baking soda	5 ml
1 tsp.	salt	5 ml
2 tsp.	cinnamon	10 ml
1/2 cup	chopped walnuts	1/8 l

Lemon Glaze:

1 cup	confectioners' sugar	1/4 l
1-1/2 tsp.	lemon juice	7-1/2 ml
1/2 tsp.	vanilla	2-1/2 ml
1 Tbs.	corn syrup	15 ml

1. Combine apples and sugar; set aside.
2. In a large mixing bowl, mix egg substitute, oil and vanilla. Add dry ingredients alternately with apple mixture. Stir in walnuts.
3. Pour into a 9" tube pan. Microwave at FULL POWER 8-10 minutes.
4. Mix ingredients for Lemon Glaze. Drizzle over cake.

Makes 1 cake.

Microwave time: 8-10 minutes
Conventional range time: 45-50 minutes at 350°

Apple Strudel

The lovelorn lady of Solomon's *Song of Songs* writes, "I am the rose of Sharon, the lily of the valleys. As the lily among thorns, so is my love among the trees of the wood, so is my beloved among the songs. I sat down under his shadow with great delight, and his fruit was sweet to my taste. He brought me to the banqueting house, and his banner over me was love. Stay me with flagons, comfort me with apples: for I am sick of love."

For those who are comforted by apples, here is a fine recipe.

4	fillo or strudel leaves (or pastry dough) at room temperature	
1/4 cup	melted butter	1/16 l
1/4-1/2 cup	fine bread crumbs	1/16-1/8 l
3	apple chunks	
1/2 cup	sugar	1/8 l
1/4 cup	raisins	1/16 l
1/2 cup	chopped dried apricots	1/8 l
1/4 cup	chopped nuts	1/16 l
	grated rind of lemon	
	juice of 1/2 lemon	
	cinnamon and sugar	

1. Unfold 1-2 fillo leaves, depending on the thickness you prefer.
2. Place leaves on a damp cloth to keep from drying up while you are working.
3. Heat butter in microwave oven for 30 seconds.
4. Paint the first leaf with melted butter. Place the second leaf on top of the first and paint it with butter and sprinkle bread crumbs over it.
5. Mix fruits, sugar, nuts, lemon rind and juice. Place half this mixture on edge of dough nearest you in one strip. Roll like a jelly-roll. Place first strudel roll in a buttered 9" baking dish.
6. Paint top lightly with melted butter, cinnamon and sugar.
7. Prepare the other two leaves the same with the remaining ingredients. Bake each roll separately 8-9 minutes, basting top once with butter.

Makes 2 strudel rolls, about 16 pieces when cut.

Microwave time: 8-1/2 to 10-1/2 minutes
Conventional range time: 35 minutes at 375°

Knobby Apple Squares

3 Tbs.	butter or margarine	45 ml
1/2 cup	white sugar	1/8 l
1/2 cup	brown sugar	1/8 l
2 cups	flour	1/2 l
1	egg	
1 tsp.	vanilla	5 ml
1 tsp.	baking soda	5 ml
1/2 tsp.	cinnamon	2-1/2 ml
1/2 tsp.	nutmeg	2-1/2 ml
1-1/2 cups	chopped apple	3/8 l

1. Cream together butter, sugars, egg and vanilla.

2. Add dry ingredients and chopped apple.

3. Spread in a greased glass or ceramic pan. Microwave at FULL POWER 6-8 minutes.

Variation: Add 1/4 cup (1/16 l) chopped nuts or raisins. Bake 1 minute longer.

Serves 8-10.

Microwave time: 6-8 minutes
Conventional range time: 30-40 minutes at 350°

Peach Tart

1-9"	frozen pie shell	23 cm
1/3 cup	sugar	1/12 l
4	fresh peach halves	
1	egg yolk	
2 Tbs.	heavy cream	30 ml
1 tsp.	apricot liqueur	5 ml

1. Remove frozen pie shell from tin and place in buttered pie plate. Sprinkle bottom of shell with sugar.

2. Cover sugar with peach halves, cut-side-down, the halves overlapping in a spiral from the center. Microwave at FULL POWER 5 minutes.

3. In another bowl, beat egg yolk with cream and liqueur and pour over pie. Heat at FULL POWER 5 minutes more.

Variation: Substitute dark, sweet, pitted cherries for the peaches. Substitute cognac for the apricot liqueur.

Serves 4-6.

Microwave time: 10 minutes
Conventional range time: 30 minutes at 350°

Frosted Daiquiri Pie

1-1/2 cups	chocolate wafers, crumbed	3/8 l
1/3 cup	sugar	1/12 l
1/3 cup	butter	1/12 l
1/2 cup	water	1/8 l
1/3 cup	lime juice (2 limes)	1/12 l
1/3 cup	sugar	1/12 l
1 Tbs.	unflavored gelatin	15 ml
2	eggs, separated	
4-5 drops	green food coloring	
	grated peel of one lime	
1/4 cup	white rum	1/16 l
3 Tbs.	sugar	45 ml
1 cup (or)	whipping cream	1/4 l
1 4-1/2 oz. carton	frozen whip	130 g

1. Melt butter in a 9" pie plate in microwave oven 45 seconds.

2. Combine cookie crumbs and sugar in a small bowl until well-blended.

3. Stir cookie mixture into butter.

4. Press mixture onto the bottom and sides of the pie plate.

5. Place uncovered in microwave oven and heat 2 minutes or until crust reaches a crunchy texture. Do not overcook! Allow to cool.

6. In a large bowl, combine water, lime juice, sugar, gelatine, and beaten egg yolks. Place in microwave oven and cook at FULL POWER 3 minutes, uncovered. Stir occasionally. If mixture boils, it may curdle. If so, just beat until it is smooth again.

7. Stir in green food coloring, grated lime peel, and rum.

8. Cool mixture; allow to thicken but not set completely.

9. Beat egg whites until frothy; gradually beat in 3 Tbs. of sugar and continue beating until mixture holds in stiff peaks.

10. Using a large bowl, whip cream and fold in gelatine mixture and beaten egg whites. Pour into pastry shell.

11. Refrigerate at least 4 hours before serving.

Makes 1 pie.

Microwave time: 5 minutes

Conventional range time: 10-15 minutes

It is part of a wise man to feed himself with moderate pleasant food and drink, and to take pleasure with perfumes, with the beauty of growing plants, dress, music, sports, and theatres, and other places of this kind which may use without any hurt to his fellows.

— Benedict (Baruch) Spinoza

Nana's Rhubarb Pie

2 9 inch	frozen pie shells and tops	23 cm each
2 cups	fresh rhubarb, cut into 1/2" slices	1/2 l
1/2 cup	brown sugar	1/8 l
1/2 cup	white sugar	1/8 l
1-1/2 heaping Tbs.	cornstarch	22-1/2 ml
1	orange, whose rind is grated and juice	
1/8 tsp.	salt	5/8 ml
3 tsp.	butter	15 ml
1/4 cup	sugar	1/16 l
2 Tbs.	cinnamon	30 ml
1	egg, beaten	

1. Transfer one frozen pie shell from tin foil to plate. Microwave at FULL POWER 3 minutes. Set aside to cool.

2. Mix the rhubarb, sugars, cornstarch, orange rind and juice, and salt together and pour into pie shell. Dot with teaspoons of butter.

3. Cut top pie shell into 3/4-inch wide strips and form a latice top. Press edges or flute together with bottom crust. Mix beaten egg, cinnamon and sugar together and pour over lattice top. Microwave at FULL POWER 6-8 minutes.

Variation: Add 1/2 cup (1/8 l) halved fresh strawberries and reduce cut rhubarb by 1/2 cup (1/8 l).

Serves 6-8.

Microwave time: 9-11 minutes
Conventional range time: 45-50 minutes at 350°

Dinners for Two

CHAPTER 9

Much food preparation time can be saved by using a recipe for four and freezing half. At a future date, you will have your dinner ready and need only pop it into the microwave oven for full restoration and even enhancement of its original flavor. The following entrees and desserts will supply you with ideas around which you can build a menu.

ENTREE: BEEF BOURGUINON
DESSERT: BAKED PEARS IN WINE, BROWNIES

Beef Bourguignon:

1 Tbs.	shortening	15 ml
1/2 lb.	beef, cut into 1-inch cubes	227 g
1/4 cup	flour	1/16 l
	salt and pepper	
1/4 tsp.	thyme	1-1/4 ml
1	bay leaf	
1 8-oz. can	whole onions (drained) or	227 g
6 small	white onions	
1 8-oz. can	whole, peeled tomatoes	227 g
1 4-oz. can	mushrooms	115 g
1 Tbs.	bacon bits	15 ml
1/2 cup	dry red wine	1/8 l

1. Preheat browning dish 5 minutes. Add shortening and heat 45 seconds.

2. Combine salt and pepper with flour and coat sides of meat with mixture.

3. Brown meat in microwave oven and cook at FULL POWER 3 minutes, turning once.

4. Add thyme, bay leaf, onions, tomatoes, mushrooms, bacon bits and wine. Cook for another 2 minutes at FULL POWER.

5. Stir, cover and cook at FULL POWER for about 10 minutes, or until heated through.

Serves 2.

Microwave time: 20 minutes
Conventional range time: 35 minutes

Baked Pears in Wine:

2	firm pears	
1/3 cup	orange marmelade or apricot jam	1/12 l
1/4 cup	light vermouth	1/16 l
2 Tbs.	butter or margarine	30 ml

1. Peel, quarter, and core pears.

2. Cut into 1/2" (1-1/4 cm) strips.

3. Arrange in two dishes that will go right to the table.

4. Mix the marmalade and vermouth in a small bowl and pour this mixture over the pears.

5. Place in microwave oven and cook at FULL POWER 5 minutes.

Serves 2

Microwave time: 5 minutes
Conventional range time: 20 minutes

Brownies

These are delicious plain, served warm with ice cream and fudge sauce, or cooled and frosted with chocolate icing or a simple confectioners sugar dusting. Freeze and use as needed.

2 1-oz. squares	unsweetened chocolate	56 g
1/2 cup	butter	1/8 l
3	eggs, well-beaten	
1 cup	sugar	1/4 l
3/4 cup	bread flour	3/16 l
1/2 tsp.	baking powder	2-1/2 ml
1/2 tsp.	salt	2-1/2 ml
1/2 tsp.	cinnamon	2-1/2 ml
1 tsp.	vanilla	5 ml
1/2 cup	chopped walnuts	1/8 l

1. Melt butter and chocolate in measuring cup 1 minute in microwave oven.

2. Add sugar slowly to beaten eggs.

3. Add sifted flour with baking powder, salt and cinnamon.

4. Add melted butter/chocolate mixture and vanilla.

5. Add nuts.

6. Spread in shallow pan 7 x 12". Let stand 10-15 minutes.

7. Microwave at FULL POWER 6 minutes.

Serves 8.

Microwave time: 6 minutes
Conventional range time: 20 minutes at 350°

Whether you are sharing food romantically or moderately with a loved one or a friend, a dinner for two should be an oasis from the tensions of everyday life.

> A book of Verses underneath the Bough,
>   A jug of Wine, a Loaf of Bread — and Thou
>   Beside me singing in the Wilderness —
>   Oh, Wilderness were Paradise enow!

> — Edward Fitzgerald

ENTREE: BACK BAY SCALLOPS, BROCOLLI PARMESAN
DESSERT: DEEP-DISH CHERRY PIE

Back Bay Scallops

Shells can be purchased for baking individual servings. They will go from the microwave oven to the table and look very appealing.

1/2 lb.	fresh bay scallops or frozen scallops	227 g
1/4 cup	flour	1/16 l
1/2 tsp.	salt	2-1/2 ml
1/8 tsp.	pepper	5/8 ml
1/4 cup	milk or cream	1/16 l
1-1/2 Tbs.	butter or margarine	22-1/2 ml
	Bread crumbs or cracker crumbs	

1. Wash scallops in cold water. Drain and pat dry on paper towel.
2. Roll in seasoned flour.
3. Grease shells. Fill each shell with floured scallops.
4. Add milk to each shell.
5. Place in microwave oven and cook at FULL POWER 5 minutes.
6. Sprinkle crumbs on top. Dot with margarine or butter.
7. Place in microwave oven and heat at FULL POWER another 5 minutes.

Serves 2.

Microwave time: 10 minutes
Conventional range time: 30 minutes at 325°

Broccoli Parmesan

1 lb.	fresh broccoli	1/2 k
1 Tbs.	butter or margarine	15 ml
1/2 tsp.	garlic salt	25 ml
	Parmesan cheese, grated	

1. Trim broccoli stalks and split into pieces about 1/4 inch thick. Arrange in circle in casserole, placing stalks toward edge of dish and flowers toward center.
2. Microwave on FULL POWER 5-6 minutes, or until broccoli is just tender.
3. Heat butter and garlic salt in a 1-cup liquid measure 1/2 minute. Drizzle over broccoli. Sprinkle with cheese.

Serves 2.

Microwave time: 7 minutes
Conventional range time: 10 minutes

Deep-Dish Cherry Pie:

1 16-oz. can	water-packed, pitted, tart red cherries	454 g
1/2 cup	sugar	1/8 l
4 Tbs.	all-purpose flour	60 ml
1/4 tsp.	cinnamon	1-1/4 ml

Crunchy Oatmeal Topping:

1/2 cup	quick-cooking oatmeal, uncooked	1/8 ml
1/2 cup	brown sugar	1/8 l
4 Tbs.	all-purpose flour	60 ml
5 Tbs.	butter or margarine	75 ml

1. Pour liquid from cherries into an oven-proof bowl.
2. Dissolve sugar, flour, and cinnamon in cherry liquid.
3. Place in microwave oven and heat at FULL POWER 1 minute or until mixture comes to a boil. Stir.
4. Add cherries.
5. Prepare Crunchy Oatmeal Topping in another bowl.
6. Into two 5-inch soufflé dishes, pour cherry mixture. Add topping. Place in microwave oven and cook at FULL POWER 6 minutes.

Makes 2 small pies, 2-4 servings.

Microwave time: 7 minutes
Conventional range time: 25-30 minutes

ENTREE: EASY BARBECUED CHICKEN BREASTS,
         CARROTS GOURMET
DESSERT: VANILLA ICE CREAM WITH JAVA SAUCE

Easy Barbecued Chicken Breasts:

The use of honey in the sauce is particularly appropriate in a dinner for two. Since ancient times, honey has been of significance to men in religion and romance. The Hindus believed their god of love had a bow whose string comprised a chain of bees. These bees symbolized the sweetness and sting of love. The Greek god of love, Amor, dipped his arrows in honey. And, Mohammed taught that the bee was the only creature to whom the Lord spoke directly. Combined with the sacred moon, honey became *honeymoon,* which denoted the first month of marriage, thought to be the sweetest.

1 12-oz. bottle	chili sauce	340 g
1 8-oz. jar	honey	227 g
1	medium onion, sliced	
2 (1/2 lb.)	chicken breasts	454 g
1	green pepper, sliced	

1. Combine chili sauce, honey, and onion.

2. Place the chicken breasts in a baking dish or platter, cover with the sauce, and cook at FULL POWER in microwave oven 10 minutes.

3. Add green pepper and cook at FULL POWER another 2 minutes or until tender.

Variation: Substitute 1/4 cup (1/16 l) slivered almonds for green pepper. Sprinkle almonds over sauce and chicken. Heat at FULL POWER 2 minutes.

Serves 2.

Microwave time: 12 minutes
Conventional range time: 30 minutes at 350°

Carrots Gourmet:

1 cup	carrots, peeled and thinly sliced	1/4 l
	Juice and grated rind of half a small orange	
1-1/2 tsp.	lemon juice	8 ml
2	scallions, diced	
	Salt and pepper, to taste	
1-1/2 tsp.	butter or margarine	8 ml
1-1/2 tsp.	heavy cream	8 ml
	Dash of nutmeg	

1. Place carrots in 1-quart oven-proof bowl.

2. Add orange juice, rind and lemon juice; stir. Add scallions, salt, pepper and butter.
3. Cover and microwave at FULL POWER 5 minutes, or until tender.
4. Add cream and nutmeg and puree until creamy.
Serves 2.

Microwave time: 5-7 minutes
Conventional range time: 10-15 minutes

Java Sauce:

This sauce was originally inspired by a flirtatious bachelor who owned an ice cream store. No one seemed able to pry the recipe out of him — not even my charming, widowed friend. Piqued by his secretiveness, she spent hours and hours creating her own version of Java Sauce. Nevertheless, she still wants to know his recipe. She vows that, in the next life, she will be such a devastating Delilah that he will be compelled to give her his recipe. Fortunately, we do not have to wait for my friend's reincarnation. Her Java Sauce recipe is totally satisfying. Use it over ice cream, cakes, and puddings. If any is left over, store in refrigerator. Reheat and stir vigorously when next you use it.

2 cups	dark brown sugar	1/2 l
2/3 cup	dark corn syrup	1/6 l
1 Tbs.	instant coffee	15 ml
2 Tbs.	water	30 ml
2/3 cup	evaporated milk	1/6 l
(1 5-1/3 oz. can)		
1/2 tsp.	salt	2-1/2 ml
1/3 cup	butter, room temperature	1/12 l
1 tsp.	vanilla	5 ml
1/4 cup	dark rum	1/16 l

1. Combine sugar, corn syrup, coffee, water, and milk in a 2-qt. container. Stir until dissolved.
2. Add butter.
3. Heat in microwave oven 10-12 minutes, or until candy thermometer registers 240°. Remember to remove container to test temperature outside oven. Stir about every 4 minutes. This sauce boils up very fast and very high. Be sure to use a large enough container. The time will vary slightly with the size of the container.
4. Remove from microwave oven and beat two full minutes with electric beater until smooth and thick, adding rum and vanilla.
5. Store in refrigerator in covered container. Heat to serve.

Makes 2 - 2-1/2 cups.

Microwave time: 10-12 minutes.
Conventional range time: 20-40 minutes.

Kids' Cookery

CHAPTER 10

Sukiyaki

This dish looks as if you have been preparing it since dawn. But it is simply your addition of beef to a convenience package of oriental vegetables and sauce mix for stir-fry sukiyaki. Serve over a bed of rice. Reheat the next day for an even more flavorful dish.

1 29-3/4 oz. pkg.	oriental vegetables	.845 k
1 lb.	steak, round or flank	454 g
1 Tbs.	salad or cooking oil	15 ml
3/4 cup	cold water	3/8 l

1. Cut steak into paper thin slices or ask an adult to do this. Slightly frozen meat cuts easier.

2. Place browning dish in microwave oven. Preheat for 4 minutes. Remove from oven. Slowly add oil, making sure your face and hands do not get spattered. Return pan to oven and slowly add steak pieces, being careful of spatters.

3. Cook in microwave oven at FULL POWER 4 minutes, turning steak pieces once.

4. Add water and sukiyaki sauce mix to pan and heat at FULL POWER 4 minutes more or until mixture boils. Stir occasionally.

5. Drain oriental vegetables and add to meat mixture. Mix outside oven thoroughly. Place in oven. Cook 1-2 minutes more at FULL power or until sukiyaki is heated through. Allow for 5-10 minutes standing time before serving.

Variation: Substitute 1 lb. of lean ground beef for the steak, but be sure to pour off the excess fat when browning the ground beef.

Serves 4.

Microwave time: 13-14 minutes
Conventional range time: 25-35 minutes.

Chicken Fantastique

This is an easy, elegant way to fix chicken when it's your turn to prepare dinner.

3-lb.	frying chicken, cut up	1.4 k
	salt and pepper	
Fantastique Sauce:		
1 8-oz. bottle	French or Russian salad dressing	240 g
1 10-oz jar	apricot jam or preserves	300 g
1 1-oz. package	dried onion soup mix	28.4 g

1. Salt and pepper chicken parts. Place in a large, 3-qt. casserole. Puncture skin of chicken in a few places.
2. Mix ingredients for topping in a bowl and pour over the chicken.
3. Cook at FULL POWER 18-20 minutes.

Serves 4-6.

Microwave time: 18-20 minutes
Conventional range time: 45 minutes at 350°

Hiker's Chops

My daughter wraps these cold and carries them in her backpack over hill and dale.

2 cups	cooked soybeans, ground or mashed	1/2 l
1 cup	cooked rice	1/4 l
2 Tbs.	chopped onion	30 ml
2	eggs	
1/2 tsp.	salt	2-1/2 ml
1/2 tsp.	celery salt	2-1/2 ml
1 cup	soft whole wheat bread crumbs	1/4 l
1 tsp.	soy sauce	5 ml

1. Mix all the ingredients together. Form into patties or chops and arrange in a circle on a 9-inch baking dish.
2. Place in microwave oven and heat at FULL POWER 10-12 minutes.

Serves 4-6.

Microwave time: 10-12 minutes
Conventional range time: 25 minutes at 350°

Hollywood Eggs

Sometimes this is called "Toad in the Hole" or "Bull's Eye." A friend prefers this more sophisticated title because that is what her older sister, home from college the first Christmas, called it. It evoked to my friend all the glamour of life away from home, aiming at the stars.

1 Tbs.	butter	15 ml
1 slice	bread	
1	egg	

1. Place butter in small 5 to 7" plate in microwave oven and heat for 45 seconds at FULL POWER or until melted.

2. With a glass, shape a circle in the center of the slice of bread and cut it out. Put bread into butter, coating it on either side. Place in center of dish.

3. Break egg into hole in cut-out center of bread. (Puncture the yolk.) Place in microwave oven and cook at FULL POWER 30 seconds - 1 minute. Remove from oven before the white has set because the steam will cook the white.

Serves 1.

Microwave time: 1 minute 30 seconds-2 minutes
Conventional range time: 5-7 minutes

Whole Wheat Muffins

1/4 cup	butter or margarine	1/16 l
1/4 cup	honey	1/16 l
1 cup	yogurt*	1/4 l
1	egg	
1 cup	whole wheat flour	1/4 l
1/3 cup	chopped nuts	1/12 l
1/4 cup	wheat germ	1/16 l
1 tsp.	baking powder	5 ml
2 tsp.	baking soda	5 ml
1/2 tsp.	salt	2-1/2 ml

1. Heat together butter and honey in medium-size mixing bowl 30 seconds on FULL POWER.

2. Stir in yogurt and egg; add combined remaining ingredients; mix just until dry ingredients are moistened.

3. Fill 12 paper muffin cups 2/3 full; place 6 filled muffin cups in microwave muffin dish or baking cups.

4. Cook 3 minutes 30 seconds on ROAST; (70% of power), repeat with remaining batter. Serve warm.

Makes 1 dozen muffins

*See recipe for Yogurt in Other Uses chapter.

Microwave time: 4 min.
Conventional range time: 30-40 min. at 375°

Banana Boats

This is a challenge for anyone who is skillful at separating egg white from egg yolk. Beating the egg white to a froth calls for something my younger son used to think was a product sold in the supermarket — "elbow grease."

1	banana	
1 tsp.	sugar and cinnamon mixed	5 ml
1 tsp.	sugar	5 ml
1 tsp.	lime juice	5 ml
1	egg	

1. Slit inner side of banana lengthwise. Do not cut through bottom of the peel.
2. Sprinkle sugar and cinnamon mixture and juice over the cut banana.
3. Let banana stand while you separate egg white from yolk.
4. In a 1-qt. bowl or blender, beat egg white to a peak to form "sails."
5. Add sugar to egg white.
6. Spread egg white mixture over the open side of the banana like sails.
7. Place in a small 7" baking dish in microwave oven and heat at FULL POWER 30 seconds.
8. Let stand a few minutes before tasting.

Serves 1-2.

Variation: Use a peach and make a peach puff.

Microwave time: 30 seconds
Conventional range time: 5 minutes at 350°

Candied Apples

1 14-oz. bag	light caramels	400 g
2 Tbs.	water	30 ml
5 medium-sized	apples, washed and dried	
5	wooden sticks	
1/2 cup	coconut or	1/8 l
1/2 cup	chopped nuts (optional)	1/8 l

1. Take paper off caramels and place caramels in a deep, 2-qt., heat-resistant, non-metallic bowl. Add water and place in microwave oven and heat 3-4 minutes at FULL POWER or until caramels melt. Remove from oven.

2. Push sticks into the center of each apple. Dip each apple in hot caramel mixture, turning to coat apple evenly.

3. On wax paper, spread coconut or nuts and roll each apple in mixture until well-coated. Place apples on buttered wax paper to cool. If caramel hardens, reheat for 45 seconds and continue working.

Makes 5 candied apples.

Microwave time: 3-4 minutes
Conventional range time: 12-14 minutes

Peanut Butter Fudge

This is a blond and creamy fudge. Easy to make.

1-1/2 cups	white sugar	3/8 l
1 cup	brown sugar	1/4 l
2/3 cup	canned evaporated milk	1/7 l
7 oz. jar	peanut butter	195 g
7 oz. jar	marshmallow whip	195 g
1 tsp.	vanilla	5 ml

1. Combine sugars and milk in a deep, 2-qt. bowl. Place in microwave oven and heat 2-3 minutes at FULL POWER or until it is heated to a rolling boil. Remove from oven.

2. Stir in rest of ingredients and blend thoroughly. Pour into a buttered 10" shallow dish. Chill in refrigerator for at least 2 hours or until fudge is firm enough to eat. Cut into squares.

Candied Citrus Peel

The next time you eat an orange or squeeze a lemon, save the peeling. Recycle into Candied Citrus Peel

2 cups	citrus fruit peel	1/2 l
1-1/2 cups	water	3/8 l
1/2 tsp.	baking soda	2-1/2 ml
1/4 cup	water	1/16 l
1 cup	sugar	1/4 l

1. Peel oranges, lemons, and grapefruit by scoring outside of fruit in quarter sections.
2. Cut into thin strips until there are 2 cups of strips. Place in deep, 2-qt. bowl.
3. Cover with 1-1/2 cups water and 1/2 teaspoon baking soda.
4. Bring to a boil in microwave oven – about 5-6 minutes.
5. Remove and rinse in colander in cold water.
6. Return to deep casserole.
7. Add 1/4 cup water and 1/2 cup sugar.
8. Boil until syrup is absorbed, about 6 minutes, stirring at least twice. All strips need to be well-coated with syrup. The peel should also have a transparent look.
9. Spread on shallow plate or paper towel and coat with granulated sugar while still warm.
10. Turn over several times to give sugary, crusty coating. Variation: 1. Add a bit of ground cinnamon, ginger or allspice for piquant flavor. 2. Strips may also be dipped in chocolate coating. 3. Candied nuts (pecans, almonds, peanuts, and cashews). Begin with Step 7. Use same syrup and boil nuts for 4 minutes. Then prepare wax paper with sugar sprinkled on it. Roll nuts in sugar untill well-coated. Remove to a plate to dry.

Makes 2 cups.

Microwave time: 7-8 minutes
Conventional range time: 15-20 minutes

Fortune Cookies

These are lots of fun to prepare. Type or write fortunes on strips of paper, 3 x 1" in size. Kids enjoy creating fortunes that can apply to their age group. My son, at 15, created messages such as: "you will inherit money soon from Howard Hughes," "Yield, it's more fun," and "Don't go near the water without a safety pin." After the cookies have baked, curl them while still warm over a wood spoon handle, and insert a fortune in each, letting part of the paper project. Pinch the ends of the cookies closed, while cookie is still warm. If they cool too quickly, return to oven for 15 seconds.

1	unbeaten egg white	
1/4 cup	sugar	1/16 l
1/4 cup	flour	1/16 l
1/2 tsp.	vanilla	2-1/2 ml
	cinnamon	
1/8 cup	butter	1/32 l

1. Combine unbeaten egg white and sugar in a small, 1-qt. bowl and mix well until sugar is dissolved. Stir in, one at a time, the other dry ingredients. Then beat until well-blended.

2. Melt butter in a small, 1-qt. bowl in microwave oven, 15 seconds.

3. Remove from oven and beat batter into the butter.

4. Drop the dough by teaspoonsful, well apart, onto a lightly greased baking dish. Microwave at FULL POWER 3 minutes. (9-12 cookies can bake at once.)

5. Let stand only one minute because it is necessary to curl cookie while warm. The top of the cookie will be the outside of the cookie; the underneath part will be folded inward with the message.

6. Repeat Steps 4 and 5 for next batch.

Makes 1 to 1-1/2 dozen.

Microwave time: 3 minutes, 15 seconds – 3 minutes, 30 seconds per batch
Conventional range time: 12-15 minutes at 350°

Double Chocolate Fondue

This is an excellent party food. Bring the hot chocolate fondue to the table and place around it bowls of the following foods with toothpicks for dipping each piece into the fondue: pound cake, cut into cubes; angel food cake, cut into cubes; animal crackers; ladyfingers; banana slices; apple chunks; drained canned pineapple chunks; strawberries, drained maraschino cherries; dried fruits; mints; nuts; and marshmallows. You may also serve bowls of shredded coconut and chopped nuts for coating the dipped sweets. Be sure to allow for standing time so that your tongue is not burned!

1 8-oz. package	semisweet chocolate, broken into pieces	227 g
1 8-oz. package	milk chocolate, broken into pieces	227 g
1/2 cup	milk	1/8 l
1 14-oz. can	sweetened condensed milk	397 g
1/4 cup	sugar	1/16 l

1. Combine all ingredients in a medium-sized, 2-qt., oven-proof bowl or serving dish.
2. Heat at FULL POWER, uncovered in microwave oven 4-5 minutes or until melted. Stir occasionally.
3. Let stand 5 minutes. Then serve surrounded by bowls of food with toothpicks for dipping.
4. If sauce sets, reheat in microwave oven for 1 minute. You may need to add a bit more milk for proper consistency.

Makes 50-60 pieces.

Microwave time: 4-5 minutes
Conventional range time: 15-40 minutes

Molasses Popcorn Balls

6-8 cups	popped corn	1-1/2 to 2 l
NOTE: Use microwave popper only		
1 cup	sugar	1/4 l
1/3 cup	light or dark corn syrup	1/12 l
1/8 cup	water	1/32 l
3 Tbs.	butter or margarine	45 ml
2 Tbs.	molasses	30 ml
1/2 tsp.	salt	2-1/2 ml

1. Have corn already popped and measured in buttered bowl.
2. In deep, 3-qt. bowl, blend sugar, corn syrup, and water. Place in microwave oven and heat at FULL POWER 12-14 minutes, stirring twice. Test candy OUTSIDE OF OVEN either by a candy thermometer to see if it has reached 295-300° F., or by dropping syrup from a teaspoon in a glass of cold water to see if it forms a hard ball. If syrup needs more cooking, **remove candy thermometer** and return to microwave oven for additional cooking.
3. If syrup is hard enough, remove from oven, add butter or margarine, molasses, and salt. Mix well.
4. Pour over popcorn. With 2 forks, mix quickly until kernels are evenly coated.
5. Roll mixture into balls when cool enough to handle. When balls are cold, wrap in wax paper twisting both ends closed.

Variation: Instead of popped corn, use 6-8 cups dry cereal, or all of one kind of mixed cereals. Follow directions for Mollasses Popcorn Balls.

Makes 2 dozen balls.

Microwave time: 12-18 minutes
Conventional range time: 30-40 minutes

S'Mores

graham crackers
marshmallows
milk chocolate candy bars

1. For each S'More, place 2 squares of milk chocolate candy bar on a graham cracker.
2. Top with a large marshmallow, and then another cracker.
3. Wrap in paper napkin.
4. Heat in microwave oven at FULL POWER until marshmallow melts. Be careful not to overcook. Marshmallows can turn dark and scorch in center before dark spots show on the outside.

Microwave time: 15 seconds per S'More
Conventional range time: 15-20 minutes at 300°

Seven Minute Brownies

2 cups	graham cracker crumbs	1/2 l
1 6-oz. package	semisweet chocolate pieces	170 g
1/2 cup	chopped nutmeats	1/8 l
1-1/3 cups (1 can)	sweetened condensed milk	1/3 l

1. Mix together graham cracker crumbs, chocolate pieces, and nutmeats in lightly greased 8″ square baking dish.
2. Stir in milk. Spread evenly.
3. Microwave at FULL POWER 7 minutes.
4. Let cool a few minutes in dish. Cut in squares. Dust with confectioners' sugar. If you wish to create a design with this sugar, place a lace doily over the brownies. Dust doily with sugar which will fall through the holes to create a design.

Makes 1-1/2 dozen.

Microwave time: 7 minutes
Conventional range time: 20 minutes at 325°

Lollipops

1 cup	sugar	1/4 l
1/2 cup	light corn syrup	1/8 l
1/4 tsp.	cream of tartar	1-1/4 ml
2 Tbs.	water	30 ml
	coloring if desired	

Any one of the following flavoring oils *or* flavoring extracts:

Flavoring Oils: 1/2 teaspoon (2-1/2 ml) of cinnamon, orange, clove, or lemon

Flavoring Extracts: 2 teaspoons (10 ml) of vanilla, cherry, or orange; 2 Tablespoons (30 ml) of raspberry.

6-10 wooden sticks, or toothpicks

1. Combine first 5 ingredients in a deep, 2-qt. bowl.

2. Place in microwave oven and heat at FULL POWER 2-3 minutes or until sugar is dissolved and boiling starts. Stir occasionally. Heat to 310° F. on a candy thermometer TESTING OUTSIDE OF OVEN.

3. Add flavoring oils or extracts, and coloring.

4. Arrange sticks on an oily surface, such as a buttered marble slab or cookie sheet, and pour candy over one end of each stick. Decorate with life savers and jelly beans, if you wish, while still hot. Loosen candy from oily surface as soon as it is firm in order to avoid its cracking when cold. Wrap in wax paper.

5. Store lollipops in tightly covered container in a cool place.

Makes 12 lollipops.

Microwave time: 3-5 minutes
Conventional range time: 12-15 minutes

Pep-Up Cookies

These health food cookies have 6 grams of protein in each. They were developed for the microwave oven by a Michigan microwave oven fan who says the unusual taste and texture of these cookies have to "grow" on you.

1 cup	soy flour	1/4 l
1 cup	non-fat dry milk powder	1/4 l
1/2 cup	wheat germ	1/8 l
1 cup	raisins	1/4 l
1/2 cup	chopped dates	1/8 l
2	eggs	
1 cup	creamy cottage cheese	1/4 l
2 Tbs.	honey	30 ml
2 Tbs.	water	30 ml
2 Tbs.	vegetable oil	30 ml
1 tsp.	vanilla	5 ml

1. In large bowl, mix soy flour, milk powder, wheat germ, raisins, and dates.
2. In small bowl, mix cheese, eggs, water, honey, oil and vanilla.
3. Add cheese mixture to dry ingredients and blend. Dough will be stiff. Drop by spoonfuls on a greased pan.
4. Microwave at FULL POWER 3-5 minutes or until bottoms are firm.

Makes 3 dozen cookies

Microwave time: 3-5 minutes
Conventional range time: 10-15 minutes at 325°

Freezing and Preserving

CHAPTER 11

On December 11, 1975, the Congress of the United States mandated a committee to facilitate conversion to the metric system. What the metric system will do to granmothers' homilies and advertising men's verbiage may result in either a tongue-tied nation, or, at the least, a tongue-twisted nation.

Yard changes to meter ("All wool and a meter wide"). Mile changes to kilometer ("I'd walk a kilometer for a Camel"). Drop changes to milliliter ("Good to the last milliliter"). Fahrenheit changes to Celsius (normal body temperature is 37° Celsius). Inches and pounds change to centimeters and kilograms (Miss America measures 91-63-91 centimeters and weighs 50 kilograms). Pecks and bushels change to liters ("I love you 35.24 liters and 8.8096 liters").

Still, a 454 gram or pint jar of preserves will remain a loving memory of Nature's bounty and a most appropriate gift for people who have everything.

Your microwave oven can help in the blanching of food for the freezer and in making jams, jellies, and preserves.

FREEZING

In the following chart on the next page, you will notice that the blanching times do not differ much in using either microwave ovens or conventional ranges. Nevertheless, the microwave is more convenient because the kitchen will remain cool and comfortable and you will no longer need to bring huge pots of water to boil.

Here are the steps for blanching in your microwave oven.

1. **Prepare the vegetables by washing, peeling, and slicing.**
2. **Measure only 1 pound or 1 quart of vegetables for each batch into the size casserole recommended in the chart.**
3. **Add water as recommended in the chart. Do not add salt.**
4. **Cover casserole. Heat on FULL POWER.**
5. **Stir vegetables after half of time and again after blanching. When blanched, vegetables have a bright color throughout. If the vegetables do not have an evenly bright color at minimum time on chart, stir them well and continue cooking to the maximum time.**
   See Blanching of Vegetables Chart on page 124.
6. **Plunge into ice water immediately to prevent further cooking. Spread on paper towels to remove excess moisture. Blot with additional towels.**
7. **Package in freezing containers; label each with the amount, name of food, and date.**

In microwave blanching, do not blanch large volumes of food at once. The amount shown on the chart is the maximum volume advisable. Cool quickly in ice water. Wrap or store in moisture-vapor proof freezer containers.

Home canning is not recommended for microwave ovens. Microwave cooking goes to boiling temperatures but no further as long as water is still in the utensil. Therefore, a pressure cooker set at 10 pounds pressure for 240° still provides the most effective method of canning.

Blanching of Vegetables Chart

Vegetable	Amount	Casserole Size	Amount of Water	Microwave Time in Minutes
Asparagus	1 lb. (454 g) cut into 1-2 inch pieces	2-qt.	1/4 cup (1/16 l)	2-1/2 - 3-1/2
Beans, Green or Wax	1 lb. (454 g)	1-1/2-qt.	1/2 cup (1/8 l)	3-1/2 - 5-1/2
Broccoli (1" cuts)	1 bunch 1-1/4-1-1/2 lbs. (567-675 g)	2-qt.	1/2 cup (1/8 l)	3 - 5
Carrots	1 lb. (454 g) sliced	1-1/2 qt.	1/4 cup (1/16 l)	3-1/2 - 5-1/2
Cauliflower	1 head cut into flowerettes	2-qt.	1/2 cup (1/8 l)	3 - 5
Corn on the Cob	Corn cut from 4 ears	1-qt.	1/4 cup (1/16 l)	4 -5
Onions	4 medium quartered	1-qt.	1/2 cup (1/8 l)	2-1/2 -4
Parsnips	1 lb. (454 g) cubed	1-1/2-qt.	1/4 cup (1/16 l)	2 - 3-1/2
Peas	2 lb. (908 g)	1-qt.	1/4 cup (1/16 l)	3 - 4-1/2
Spinach	1 lb. (454 g) washed	2-qt.	none	2 -3
Squash, Summer, Yellow, Zucchini	1 lb. (454 g) sliced or cubed	1-1/2-qt.	1/4 cup (1/16 l)	2-1/2 - 4
Turnips	1 lb. (454 g) cubed	1-1/2-qt.	1/4 cup (1/16 l)	2-1/2 - 4

PRESERVING

Nothing sends a fragrance through a home as do jams, jelies, and relishes. Follow the basic recommendations, but use your own creativity in varying the flavors by adding liqueurs, spices, herbs, and flowers.

Here are the basic recommendations for preserving:

1. Have pot holders near the oven because sugar mixtures become very hot.

2. Avoid steam burns by removing the lid away from you.

3. Whenever pectin is added, be sure to add it gradually and stir in well.

4. Sterilize jars and glasses in a pot of boiling water on the conventional range. Melt parraffin in a double boiler on the range.

5. Pour jelly or preserves into hot, sterilized glasses. Wipe rims well with a cloth dipped in hot, sterilized water. Seal with hot, sterilized lids or paraffin.

Apple Jelly

2 cups	bottled unsweetened apple juice	1/2 l
3-1/2 cups	sugar	7/8 l
6 oz.	liquid fruit pectin	180 g

1. In 3-qt. casserole, stir together apple juice and sugar.

2. Cover. Place in microwave oven and heat at FULL POWER 12-14 minutes, stirring after 6 minutes, until boiling.

3. Stir in pectin, mixing thoroughly. Cover. Return to oven and continue cooking at FULL POWER 4-6 minutes or until mixture begins to boil again.

4. Let boil for 1 minute.

5. Ladle mixture into hot, sterilized jars or glasses and seal.

Makes about 3 cups.

Variations:

Mint Jelly — Before removing jelly after Step 4, add 1/8 tsp. (5/8 ml) of peppermint extract and a drop of green coloring.

Rose Geranium Jelly — Before removing jelly after Step 4, bruise 3 rose geranium leaves and pass through jelly until desired flavor is obtained. Add a drop of red coloring.

Microwave time: 17-19 minutes
Conventional range time: 30-35 minutes

Grape Jelly

1 6-oz. can	frozen grape juice concentrate, defrosted	180 g
1-3/4 oz.	powdered fruit pectin	22 g
2 cups	hot water from faucet	1/2 l
3-3/4 cups	sugar	750 g

1. In 3-qt. casserole, mix together grape juice and pectin. Stir in water.
2. Cover. Place in microwave oven and heat at FULL POWER 8-9 minutes. Stir after 4 minutes, until bubbles form around edge.
3. Add sugar and mix well. Cover. Return to microwave oven and heat at FULL POWER 6-8 minutes more, stirring well after 4 minutes, until mixture returns to boil.
4. Let boil 1 minute longer.
5. Remove from oven and skim off foam with metal spoon, stirring jam for 5 minutes. Ladle into hot sterilized glasses. Seal.

Makes 4 cups.

Microwave time: 15-18 minutes
Conventional range time: 35-40 minutes

Strawberry Jam

4-1/2 cups	washed, cleaned, crushed, fresh strawberries	1-1/8 l
1-3/4 oz.	powdered fruit pectin	52 g
7 cups	sugar	1-1/3 l

1. In 3-qt. casserole, place berries and pectin. Stir well.
2. Cover. Place in microwave oven and heat at FULL POWER 8-10 minutes until mixture is at a rolling boil
3. Add sugar to boiling mixture and stir well. Return uncovered to microwave oven and heat at FULL POWER 8-10 minutes, stirring after 5 minutes, until mixture reaches a full rolling boil.
4. Let boil 1 minute longer.
5. Remove from oven and skim off foam with metal spoon, stirring jam for 5 minutes. Ladle into hot sterilized glasses. Seal.

Makes 8 cups.

Microwave time: 17-19 minutes
Conventional range time: 35-40 minutes

PICKLES AND RELISHES

Watermelon Pickles

Gone are the twelve hours of soaking! Your microwave oven will accomplish this important first step within 30 minutes.

3 qts.	white portion of water- melon, cut in chunks	3.3 l
2 cups	water	1/2 l
3 cups	sugar	3/4 l
1-1/2 cups	white vinegar	3/8 l
1 cup	water	1/4 l

Spice bag from a square of cheesecloth tied securely with string containing: 8 cloves without heads, or 2 oz. ginger root; 3 bay leaves; 2 cinnamon sticks, broken; 1 lemon, sliced thin *or* 1/2 lemon and 1/2 orange, sliced thin.

1. Cut green rind and red meat from watermelon rind. Cut rind into 1" strips. 3/4 of a medium-sized watermelon will produce the 3 qts. needed.
2. Place watermelon in 3-qt. casserole. Add water.
3. Cover. Heat in microwave oven at FULL POWER 30 minutes, stirring every 10 minutes.
4. Remove from oven and let stand while cooking syrup.
5. To cook syrup, place sugar, vinegar, water, and spice bag in 2-qt. casserole. Cover casserole and place in microwave oven to heat for 10 minutes.
6. Stir well. Continue Cooking at FULL POWER, uncovered 10 more minutes.
7. While syrup is cooking, drain water off watermelon.
8. Pour cooked syrup, including spice bag, over watermelon in 3-qt. casserole.
9. Cover. Put in microwave oven and heat at FULL POWER 35 minutes. Stir every 10 minutes. Chunks should be tender and transparent.
10. Immediately ladle hot watermelon pickles into hot sterilized jars and seal with hot, sterilized lids.

Makes 5 cups.

Microwave time: 85-95 minutes
Conventional range time: 120-140 minutes

Corn Relish

1 cup	sugar	1/4 l
2 Tbs.	cornstarch	30 ml
2 Tbs.	minced onion	30 ml
1 Tbs.	mustard seed	15 ml
1/4 tsp.	celery seed	1-1/4 ml
1/4 tsp.	turmeric	1-1/4 ml
1 cup	vinegar	1/4 l
3/4 cup	hot tap water	3/16 l
1/2 cup	pimiento, minced	1/8 l
3 12-oz. cans	whole kernel corn, drained	2.8 K

1. In 3-qt. casserole, stir together sugar, cornstarch, onion, mustard seed, celery seed and turmeric. Gradually add vinegar and water, stirring well.

2. Cover. Place in microwave oven and heat at FULL POWER 5 minutes. Stir well. Add corn and pimientoes to sauce. Cover. Return to oven and heat 15-17 minutes, at FULL POWER, stirring well after 7 minutes, until mixture boils. Stir well.

3. Ladle in prepared jars. Seal.

Makes 5-1/2 cups.

Microwave time: 20-22 minutes
Conventional range time: 40-45 minutes

Other Uses of Your Microwave Oven

CHAPTER 12

An Oregon woman who has a hectic household of four active sons, two dogs, a guinea pig, and assorted fauna and flora, depends on her microwave oven as much for its other uses as for cooking of foods. She recycles all stale buns for her pets by cooking them between paper towels to the hardness of dog biscuits; she dries flowers in commercial "kitty litter" rather than silica gel; she dries out her sons' soggy shoes to a state of mere dampness in 3 minutes; from a library of craft ideas for kids to make, she selects crafts containing neither metal nor plastic that can bake in the microwave oven in 1/4 of the conventional oven time; and she encourages her sons to be non-violent towards their "enemies" by allowing them to concoct "witches' brew," a mixture of mud, stones, dried out shoe polish, and "evil-smelling" things, that bubbles in the microwave oven with a sinister vapor!

HOW TO MAKE DRIED MUSHROOMS IN THE MICROWAVE OVEN

During my student days in Madison, Wisconsin I was an avid mushroom gatherer. Every fall and spring, I would gather various edible specimens and string them across the ceiling of my one-room apartment in order to dry them for future use. The apartment looked like a carnival tent. It would take days and days for some species to dry. Gradually I discovered that under no circumstances will inky-caps dry; that morels, those delightful spongy cone-shaped mushrooms take longer than field mushrooms or velvet-stems or elm caps to dry. 'Longer' meant, in those days, two to three days longer. Now, in microwave oven time, 'longer' means 8 minutes more.

1. Select young mushrooms that are plump and firm.
2. Slice lengthwise and lay out on a paper towel. Place in microwave oven and cook at FULL POWER for 8 minutes, turning once. Be sure that all moisture has disappeared before storing the mushrooms.
3. Dried mushrooms may be cooked as fresh. To reconstitute them, soak them in tepid water or milk for a few minutes. If some stems are tough, grind them into a powder for seasoning gravies and other dishes.

INSTRUCTIONS FOR DRYING HERBS

Some of the most tasteful toppings can be made from dried herbs. The celery leaves you might ordinarily throw away, the parsley or dill that you buy in bunches but cannot use up, and the many herbs, such as thyme, basil, tarragon, savory, mint, that you grow in your garden or on your window sill, can all be preserved by the microwave oven.

1. Select 4-6 herb branches and wash. Then place them between two paper towels.
2. Place in microwave oven and heat at FULL POWER 2-3 minutes, or until brittle and dry.
3. Remove from oven. Separate leaves from stalks and place between two sheets of wax paper. Crush with a rolling pin.
4. Put in glass or plastic jars with a firm sealed lid.

NUT ROASTING GUIDE

Use glass, not paper containers.
For shelled nuts (almonds, raw cashews and peanuts, pignolias):

1. Spread 1/2 to 1 cup of nuts in a shallow container. Place in microwave oven and heat at FULL POWER 6-10 minutes, uncovered. Stir frequently.
2. While nuts are standing, you may wish to sprinkle them with salt or teaspoon of vegetable oil and stir to coat nuts evenly.

For unshelled nuts:

Chestnuts:
1. Chestnuts should be slashed with a crisscross. Spread 1-2 dozen in a shallow container. Place in microwave oven and heat at FULL POWER for 1 minute, uncovered; stir once.
2. Let nuts stand for 5 minutes and then peel off shells. Do not let them cool too much before shelling.

Pumpkin, Sunflower, and Squash Seeds
1. Rinse fibers from seeds. Measure 1 cup of seeds. Lightly coat bottom of a shallow container with salt. Add seeds and place in microwave oven. Heat at FULL POWER 5-7 minutes or until crisp. Stir often.
2. Let stand 3 minutes.

SHELLING PECANS, ENGLISH WALNUTS, OR BRAZIL NUTS:

Place 2 cups of nuts in 1 cup water in a covered dish in microwave oven and heat at FULL POWER 1-2 minutes. Then shell. This heating process will make the nuts easy to shell.

BABY FOOD FROM SCRATCH

To make your own baby food, set aside from regular family meals meat, fish, vegetables, and fruit. Try to postpone spicing or seasoning of the family food until after you have set aside baby's portion.

Use either a strainer, food mill, or blender to prepare the food. Always use clean, freshly washed utensils.

Here are some of the foods that babies like.

Fruits: Bananas need simply be mashed with a fork. All other fruits must be peeled, cored, seeded, and cut into small pieces. Then place in a casserole, add a small amount of water, cover, and place in microwave oven and heat. Cooking time will depend on the quantity of food. Do not overcook but be sure food is soft. When it is tender, remove from oven and puree it. Place in clean jars of half-cup (for babies) or 1 cup (for Juniors) size for later use and refrigerate.

Vegetables: Carrots, peas, sweet potatoes, and zucchini are favorites. Cut these vegetables in small pieces and cook the same as for fruits. When food is soft, puree it and place in individual serving jars. Avoid beets and spinach because they may contain an excess of harmful nitrates. Broccoli, cabbage, and cauliflower may produce gas, and corn is too difficult for an infant to digest.

Meats, Poultry, Fish: Cooking these foods in the microwave oven (never frying them) will make them very digestible. After cooking, remove skin and bones. Cut up meat and puree. A blender will puree these foods quickly and well. Place in individual serving jars.

Eggs: Consult your doctor on whether your baby can eat both the white and yolk or just the yolk. If you hard-boil an egg, remember to cook it on your conventional range. (Eggs in shells explode in the microwave oven.) If you warm a shelled, hard-boiled egg in the microwave oven, prick it in several places. Custard is a favorite of babies. Follow a standard recipe, omitting sugar, nutmeg, and other spices.

Other Foods: Soup is a good choice to set aside before it has been spiced. Cottage cheese and ice cream are other favorites of babies.

Before heating, you may wish to flavor the food lightly with salt, butter, or sugar. It can then be heated to serving temperature right in the jar in which it is stored or in a serving dish. Be sure to remove metal lid before heating and cover with plastic wrap.

To reheat baby or Junior food, follow these steps:

1. Place a little over a half-cup of food (1/8 l) (equivalent to the average jar of baby food) in microwave oven covered, and heat at FULL POWER 50 seconds - 1 minute. Let stand 2 minutes so that baby will not burn his/her tongue!

2. For Junior baby food, do not grind or mash food so fine. Place a

little under 1 cup (1/4 l) of food (equivalent to the average jar of Junior food) in the microwave oven covered and heat at FULL POWER 1-2 minutes. Let stand 2-3 minutes so that baby will not burn his/her tongue!

MICROWAVE YOUR OWN YOGURT

Simply combine milk and yogurt culture, incubate it in your microwave oven (if it has a temperature probe), and in a few hours you have your own fresh, homemade yogurt. Enjoy it plain or use it in recipes. (There are some in this book.)

TIPS FOR YOGURT MAKING

*For starter, use dry yogurt culture (available at health food stores) or commercial plain yogurt containing active yogurt culture. Look at the carton label where contents are listed. Future batches can be started with your own homemade yogurt.

*Yogurt must be at room temperature before it is added to cooled milk.

*For richer, thicker yogurt, add several tablespoons of nonfat dry milk.

*Warm a clean deep bowl by rinsing with hot water or placing in a dishwasher on the drying cycle for several minutes. Use this to help maintain the temperature of the milk mixture before incubation.

*Incubation time will vary depending on the type of starter and milk. Check yogurt after 3-1/2, 4-1/2, or 5-1/2 hours of incubation.

PLAIN YOGURT

1 quart	lowfat milk	1 l
2 Tbs.	nonfat dry milk (optional)	30 ml
2 Tbs.	starter (dry culture or plain yogurt at room temperature	30 ml

1. Combine milk and nonfat dry milk in large deep bowl. Heat 12 minutes at FULL POWER or to boiling. Cool to 115°; monitor temperature with a microwave oven thermometer.

2. Combine starter with about 1/2 cup cooled milk; mix lightly until smooth.

(continued on next page)

3. Add milk mixture to remaining milk, mixing until well blended.

4. Pour into warmed, large deep bowl.

5. Place probe into milk mixture; cover with plastic wrap. Insert probe into oven. To incubate, heat to 113° on FULL POWER; hold at that temperature 3-1/2 to 5-1/2 hours. (Reset timer as needed.) Chill. Yogurt will continue to thicken as it chills.

Makes about 4 cups.

NOTE: Drain liquid from yogurt after chilled. Yogurt will become thin if liquid is stirred in.

HELP IN THE KITCHEN

Freshening stale food (chips, crackers, pretzels):

1. Place in microwave oven and heat at FULL POWER 15-30 seconds .

2. Let stand in pan 5 minutes.

Drying fresh bread for croutons or crumbs:

Cut fresh bread into croutons after removing crusts, or grind into crumbs. Place on towel in microwave oven and heat 6-7 minutes at FULL POWER. Stir a few times.

Heating brandy or other liqueurs:

1. Measure amount of brandy needed in measuring cup. Place in microwave oven and heat 10-15 seconds at FULL POWER.

2. Pour over dessert and light.

Softening brown sugar:

Place sugar in a dish with a slice of white bread or slice of apple. Cover and place in microwave oven and heat 30-45 seconds at FULL POWER, stirring once.

Defrosting frozen fruit juices:

Remove juice from can, place in pitcher and set in microwave oven and heat 30-45 seconds at FULL POWER until soft. Add water.

Warming syrup:

Heat syrup in bottle without metal cap 30-45 seconds at FULL POWER.

Warming baby bottles or jars of baby food:

Loosen cap or remove metal lid and place in microwave oven and heat 10-15 seconds at FULL POWER or until warm.

Plumping fresh citrus fuits (lemons, limes, oranges, grapefruits) before squeezing:

Place individual fruit in microwave oven for 30 seconds

Softening hardened dried fruit or gum drops:

Place fruits or candy on dish and sprinkle with 1/2 to 1 teaspoon (2-1/2 to 5 ml) of water. Cover and place in microwave oven 15-30 seconds at FULL POWER.

USES OF THE MICROWAVE OVEN AROUND THE HOUSE

1. Dry arts and crafts projects made of paper or plaster of paris on a towel Heat at 50% of power 4-1/2 to 6 minutes.

2. Loosen stuck tops of bottles, provided contents are not flammable and bottle contains no metal. Place in microwave oven with a small cup of water to balance load and heat 45 seconds - 1 minutes.

3. Soften clay by wrapping in a wet towel. Heat 3-6 minutes at FULL POWER.

4. Freshly glued pieces may be set and dried. Heat 1-2 minutes at FULL POWER.

5. Preshrink material by folding 1/2 yard (46 cm) of thoroughly wet then wrung-out material. Heat 6-8 minutes at FULL POWER, turning often.

6. Warm moist-heat pads or compresses. Heat 4-5 minutes at FULL POWER.

7. Facilitate ironing tablecloths. Dampen the cloth and place in a plastic bag. (Do not close with metal tie wrap.) Heat 30 seconds (for a 70" x 54" (178 cm by 137 cm) tablecloth) at FULL POWER. Iron immediately.

8. Warm damp wash-cloths for use after eating finger foods in a wicker basket sprinkled with lemon solution. Heat 1 minute at FULL POWER.

HOW TO MAKE DRIED FLOWERS IN THE MICROWAVE OVEN

Materials you need for drying flowers:

Flowers
Scissors
Silica-gel
Coffee cups
Wire

Green floral tape
Glue
Ice pick, toothpick
Brush

General Instructions for Making Dried Flowers

1. Choose flowers that are bright in color (yellows, red, purples are best).

2. Choose flowers with thick petals, such as chrysanthemums, asters, zinnias, pansies, carnations, roses, sunflowers, and daffodils.

3. Flowers should be very fresh, half-open and firm.

4. Avoid using flowers having long, thin petals (tulips, gladiolas, etc.) but test-dry at least one flower, to judge their ability to dry well.

5. You may place up to six flowers in the drying bowl at one time.

6. Do not put a cover on the dish while heating in the microwave oven.

7. Heating time should be as short as possible. If the flower is still soft after the recommended time, do not heat again in the microwave oven, but allow it to stand in the grains for a longer period of time.

9. When flowers seem to be dried, slowly tilt the bowl and carefully take out the flowers.

10. Silica gel grains sticking to the petals can be removed after flowers have been allowed to stand for awhile. Be careful not to break the petals when removing the last silica gel grains with a brush.

11. Spray-type coloring agents can be used to add more color to the dried flowers. Use sprays only after the flowers are completely dried. Or use dried petals to stuff a home-made sachet "pillow."

Step-by-Step Guide for Drying Flowers

1. Cut flowers to leave about 1/2 inch of stem with the blossom. Some flowers may be dried right on the stem. Test one for results and then decide which is more attractive.

2. Pour silica gel grains into a bowl and place flowers over the gel, stems down or to the side. THIS IS AN IMPORTANT STEP IN THE PROCESS: Use an ice pick, knitting needle or toothpick to separate the petals. Be sure to spread silica gel grains evenly between the petals. Take your time and fill every space between the petals and place them in the position you want them to be in when the process is completed.

3. Cover the flower completely with the silica gel. There should be absolutely no exposed petals to the air.

4. Place a cup of water in the corner of the microwave oven. (Use a heat-resistant, non-metallic measuring cup, or heat-resistant, non-metallic coffee cup.)

5. Place the flower in the microwave oven and heat 1-2 minutes at FULL POWER.

6. After heating, remove the silica-gel-covered flower from the oven, allowing it to stand in the silica gel for at least 10 to 15 minutes.

7. After flowers are dry, use the floral wire as a stem, if needed. Make a hook on one end and pull it through the center of the flower.

8. Using the floral tape, secure the flower to the wire.

9. Leaves can be dried and added to the stem of the flower, but should be dried separately.

WHAT YOU CAN MAKE WITH DRIED FLOWERS

Sachet:

Not all flowers are worth preserving for display, but most can be used for sachet.

1. Dry the flowers according to directions. When thoroughly dry, crush them.

2. Prepare a square of pretty fabric and place some of the crushed flowers in the center.

3. Sew the edges together forming a "pillow" of sachet. Decorate lace, velvet, or grosgrain edging, a monogram, or needlework.

Dried Pine Cones:

Place cones, unopened or opened, in a bowl. No silica gel is needed. Simply put the timer at 2 minutes, and remove at the end of that time. Cones that have been in snow or rain will require a few additional minutes to dry. When the cones have cooled they may be painted, used for wreaths or table decorations.

HOOKED RUG STRIPS

All hooked rug craftsmen are familiar with the art of "fading" or "blotching" wool strips of fabric to be cut into string strips for hooking. The fading process results in those soft blendable colors that mark the subtle shading of quality hooked rugs. Fading can successfully be done in the microwave oven.

1. Cut strips from any color into sizes about 2" x 8".

2. Wet and then pour powder detergent directly onto the wool cloth, spotting the powder in several areas. Do *not* cover the whole strip with powder.

3. Pack lightly into a deep, heat-resistant, non-metallic bowl or casserole. The material should fill no more than one-third of the container.

4. Cover with water and bring to a quick boil (about 3-5 minutes).

5. Watch it carefully as it can easily froth up and boil over.

6. Remove from hot water and rinse clear in cold water. Dry thoroughly.

7. Strips should be pleasantly mottled for a pleasing blend when hooked area is completed.

8. This method also works successfully with wool yarns.

DOUGH ART

For Christmas tree ornaments of stars, Santas, bells and angels, and for other holiday ornaments, such as baskets and cornucopias, here is an easy recipe that can later be colored to suit the occasion.

4 cups	flour	1 l
1 cup	salt	1/4 l
1-1/2 cups	hot water combined with instant tea or coffee to give dough a toasty color	3/8 l

1. Knead 6-8 minutes. Roll out dough and make into desired shapes. Use a needle to make several holes in each piece (to let the air escape).
2. Bake on glass tray in your microwave oven and heat 2 minutes at FULL POWER. The time will vary according to the size of the pieces.

"Bread" Baskets

1. Knead 6-8 minutes. Roll out dough to be cut into strips.
2. Cover desired dish size with plastic wrap and place covered dish inverted on a glass plate. Cut "dough" into strips and start first strip at inverted top of dish and work backwards. Do sides next and then bottom will form as you weave the strips. Seal the edges and top of basket by dampening with water and pinching down dough with a fork.
3. Place in microwave oven and heat 10-18 minutes at FULL POWER or until dough is thoroughly dry. Let cool and spray with plastic spray or paint with water colors and lacquer.

Index